Bailing Out

Bailing Out

THE HEALTHY WAY
TO GET OUT OF A BAD RELATIONSHIP
AND SURVIVE

Barry Lubetkin, Ph.D.
and
Elena Oumano, Ph.D.

PRENTICE
HALL
PRESS

NEW YORK   LONDON   TORONTO   SYDNEY   TOKYO   SINGAPORE

While the case studies described in this book are based on interviews with real persons, the names, professions, locations, and other biographical details about the participants have been changed to preserve their privacy and anonymity.

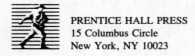

PRENTICE HALL PRESS
15 Columbus Circle
New York, NY 10023

PRENTICE HALL PRESS and colophons are registered trademarks
of Simon & Schuster, Inc.

Library of Congress Cataloging-in-Publication Data

Lubetkin, Barry.
    Bailing out : the healthy way to get out of a bad relationship and survive / Barry
Lubetkin, Elena Oumano.
        p.   cm.
    ISBN 0-13-056946-1
    1. Interpersonal relations.   2. Cognitive therapy.   I. Oumano,
Elena.   II. Title.
HM132.L83   1991
158′.24—dc20   90-33696
                                                                          CIP

Designed by Virginia Pope-Boehling

Manufactured in the United States of America

10 9 8 7 6 5 4 3 2 1

First Edition

To my wife, Ginny, who has been my greatest love and soul mate for fifteen years. And, to my children, Warren and Erica, who light up my life.

B.L.

To my son, Dr. Eric Roth.

E.O.

ACKNOWLEDGMENTS

We are especially grateful to Madeleine Morel for bringing us together and for her guidance in the initial phases of this book. We would also like to thank Diana Finch for her input. To Barry Lubetkin's partner and friend, Steven T. Fishman, Ph.D., and to our editor, Gail Winston, whose valuable advice helped shape the final manuscript, we both owe a debt of gratitude. Special thanks to Joanne Galst, Ph.D., for introducing Barry Lubetkin and Madeleine Morel. And finally, to all the people who have had the courage to bail out.

ACKNOWLEDGMENTS

CONTENTS

INTRODUCTION

Why Was This Book Written?

Fidelity or Fear?

Janet has been married to David, a successful real-estate developer, for eighteen years. They live with their two teenage sons in a luxurious estate set on the banks of the Long Island Sound. Janet has everything a woman could want, at least materially. Her days are free for shopping, the beauty parlor, the health club, lunch with friends, and courses at the adult education center. But Janet is unhappy. David is rarely home, and when he is, he and Janet have little to talk about. On Janet's fortieth birthday, David gifted her with a diamond-studded pin with the initials OBG. When Janet asked her husband what they meant, he laughed. "It means old but good," he told her. Janet said nothing. As usual, she suffered in silence. She hates the pin, but she wears it whenever David insists.

Ellen got married twenty-two years ago when she was a nineteen-year-old college student because she became pregnant. Her parents were furious and insisted that she get an abortion, live at home, and visit a psychiatrist. But Ellen's boyfriend, Nick, wanted the baby. Marriage seemed the best escape from a difficult situation, so Ellen eloped, standing up before a justice of the peace with a sinking heart. After the baby was born, Nick and Ellen started a business together. Life settled into a routine. Although they shared a child and their work, it was apparent that Ellen and her husband had little else in common and that the marriage had been a huge mistake. But Ellen soon became pregnant with a second child. Although she didn't love her husband, extricating herself from the numerous ties of work and children seemed impossible.

The children are in college now, Ellen and Nick have grown even further apart, yet they remain together out of business interests and apathy. Nothing is glaringly wrong, but nothing is right either. Ellen thinks it's simply "too late" to think about leaving.

Rosalie's relationship with Patrick actually began when Patrick, a friend of Rosalie's last boyfriend, asked if he could leave a suitcase at her apartment because he was between living situations. Patrick soon followed his suitcase. He's been there for five years. Patrick is extremely jealous. He doesn't allow Rosalie to go out unless he has approved of where she is going and with whom. He will demand a telephone number and check up to make sure she is, in fact, where she said she would be. More than a few times, he has hidden Rosalie's shoes to keep her from going out. Their arguments have escalated to the point of physical abuse. Rosalie maintains that she doesn't love Patrick and she is miserable in the situation, yet month after month goes by without her taking any action. Rosalie admits that she doesn't like to be alone. Because she has never had a good relationship with a man anyway, she says, she might as well stay with this one.

Twenty-year-old Sam has been going steady with Mindy for one year. Sam likes Mindy and enjoys her company, but he is beginning to feel increasingly stifled and dissatisfied. He realizes now that he got into the relationship this deeply because he succumbed to Mindy's pressure to make a commitment.

Sam would like to date other girls, perhaps find someone he really loves, but his guilt and fear that Mindy will fall apart if he leaves her keeps him frozen in place.

If the claims made by the mass media about the dawn of a new age of commitment are real, it is equally true that more and more people are staying together not only because they've suddenly rediscovered the bliss of monogamy but because, like the people described above, they're scared. They fear not only AIDS and other sexually transmitted diseases, but being alone. Separation and the isolation they believe inevitably follows will unleash on their partner or themselves an overwhelming flood of unhappiness. As a clinical psychologist, many of the people who come to see me* come because they are fighting the eternal misery of the cold war of a bad or indifferent relationship. Although they know they should separate, they are unable to do so. They offer up myriad rationalizations for staying, everything from the advantages of filing a joint income tax return to the children. But what child's shoulders can bear the weighty burden of keeping the parents' relationship together? "Staying together for the sake of the children" and other excuses—from the trivial to the significant—are all distractions from the unavoidable fact that many couples prefer to struggle with each other and with their own better instincts month after month, year after year, than face the pain of separation. Often, these couples finally do part long after the prolonged combat has worn them down, mentally and physically. In fact, other than incapacitating mental illness, chronic anxiety, and depression, staying together under strain is the single greatest continuing source of unhappiness people present in my practice.

Dedication is a sterling virtue, but staying with someone even when you're unhappy and unfulfilled within the relationship is not. Whatever the cause of your unhappiness and

---

Whenever the first person is used in this book, it refers to Barry Lubetkin.

dissatisfaction, staying in a bad relationship amounts to voluntary imprisonment not unlike the habitual convict who keeps committing crimes and returning to prison because the regimentation and confinement of life "inside" is easier than coping with the risks and responsibilities created by having to make his own choices in the world "outside." Remaining in the false safety of a long-dead relationship keeps you from living fully and blocks you irrevocably from the possibility of establishing a satisfying relationship with someone else.

Bailing Out Versus Free-Fall

On the other hand, "bailing out" when you know your relationship is no longer viable can be one of the most affirmative, liberating acts of one's life. Bailing out can be a wonderful growth experience *if* you use this period of your life as a time to explore, discover, and evaluate the beliefs that have determined your behavior. You can use this time to make the appropriate changes in the "life rules" that govern you to ensure a fulfilling life after you bail out and to ensure that you don't repeat your mistakes in the next relationship.

This book will help you decide whether or not you should bail out, and, if you do decide that option is best, it will lead you through the numerous small steps that comprise the process of bailing out, each one of which *by itself* is very manageable. In fact, the chapters of this book are divided according to the step-by-step process of bailing out. This book will help you to maximize your success every step of the way, including the crucial final period of the process, after you have bailed out and are at your most vulnerable. Like the parachutist jumping from the relative safety of the airplane into the vastness of space, when you leave a relationship, no matter how miserable it was, you are leaving the relative security of the known for the unknown. Like the novice jumper, you're terrified. You don't want to go, yet every instinct tells you you must go. If the aircraft of your relationship is floundering and you don't bail out, you will crash.

You may feel an initial moment of panic during the free-fall. You may forget you have a ''parachute,'' but this book will remind you that you do have a parachute—the strategies to keep you afloat, the skills to help you survive the breakup of your relationship. This book will teach you how to operate that parachute—how to use your survival strategies—more effectively. It will help you move quickly from your point of decision to bail out to that first decisive leap. Through various techniques, this book will help you realize, *on a gut level,* that being alone is not necessarily the same as loneliness. Your time alone after bailing out can be one of the most rewarding periods of your life, a breathing space during which you can redefine yourself as an individual rather than as only one-half of a couple. This period after bailing out can be precious time needed to recover from mental, emotional, perhaps even physical abuse. It can be time to enjoy peace of mind and to establish a new sense of self-worth.

Some of you may have already left a relationship. You may be fearful of dating again, of ever getting involved in another mentally and physically draining relationship and of suffering another excruciatingly painful breakup. This book can help you, too. As it leads you through the process of bailing out and toward building a new, more aware life, it will enable you to retrace the events of your past relationship. In so doing, you will profit from your mistakes by building a better understanding of yourself and by learning new, more effective strategies for coping. Knowing you are better equipped to enter into a relationship, you will be more open for a new experience and much more likely to find the happiness and fulfillment you long for.

A Case for Bailing Out
Sooner Rather than Later

The problems that normally arise in any relationship become repetitive and exhausting in a relationship that no longer works. These problems carry with them not only your present inability to communicate, but your entire history of past hurts and angers. A miserable or even a tolerable, but unsatisfying, relationship saps the time and energy required to fulfill even the most ordinary demands of daily life. This is particularly true if your daily interactions are combative or tense. Numerous other emotional problems, such as phobias, panic feelings, depression, and psychosomatic complaints, can also be traced to the demoralization brought on by an unsatisfying relationship where hope for change has disappeared, but both partners feel powerless to bail out. In fact, recent studies by Dr. Diane Chambless and others have suggested that chronic conflict over separating from a bad relationship may be one fact that leads to a devastating condition called "agoraphobia," a prevalent disabling panic disorder that can be defined as an irrational fear of leaving home and being overwhelmed by anxiety. People who suffer from agoraphobia fear that when they leave home, their bodies will somehow let them down. They suffer symptoms such as hyperventilation and tachycardia (rapid heartbeat) and generally overreact to these feelings. About 75 percent of agoraphobics are women, and a frequent source of their problem is an inability to resolve the need to get out of a bad relationship, as well as a lack of confidence in their ability to function on their own. Although numerous behavioral techniques can be useful for treating agoraphobia, the symptoms are often dramatically alleviated when the individual resolves the conflict over separation and begins to develop the wherewithal to live independently.

Of course, nothing should replace trying to resolve differences or getting help through therapy or some other kind of counseling endeavor. This book does not advocate you leave your relationship at the first sign of trouble. As long as marriages and long-term relationships are basically loving and respectful, they continue for many people to be powerful emotional stabilizers in an increasingly impersonal world. Two purposes of this book are, first, to help you identify the criteria for bailing out and, second, to recognize whether or not therapy, counseling, or "talking things out" can help the relationship.

But remember, even doctors in emergency rooms stop attempts at resuscitation once they've determined that the situation is hopeless. If you do decide that bailing out is your best option, the third goal of this book is to help you over-come the guilt, shame, fear, self-recriminations, and self-doubts that often accompany such a move—whether your relationship is a legally defined marriage or a less formal union. Our fourth goal is to prepare you for the separation in such a way that when you do bail out, you can make a smooth jump and land squarely on your feet on solid terrain.

Therapists and Bailing Out

Before we go any further, it is important to note that one problem with couples therapy and the issue of bailing out is that some therapists are gun-shy about raising the separation alternative. They have the irrational idea that practicing mari-tal therapy automatically sets them on a mission to save the relationship. Although there are comparatively few lawsuits against psychotherapists, one of the most common complaints couples make is that they feel the therapist engineered their breakup by bringing to light their submerged conflicts. For this additional reason, some therapists and counselors may be reluctant to bring up the subject of bailing out as a viable solution.

When I first see a couple, I point out to them that if after an honest effort we all agree their relationship is damaged beyond repair, individual sessions will follow with each partner in which we work toward a separation. If either reports having a lover and that she is just going through the motions of saving the relationship and really doesn't want it to continue, or if it becomes apparent that one partner is very disturbed, or that there are irreconcilable differences, I will suggest the couple consider separation as one option.

Cognitive Behavior Therapy and Bailing Out

Cognitive behavior therapy is a mode of psychotherapy that has been scientifically demonstrated to be effective in alleviating many emotional and behavioral ills. But it has not as yet been systematically applied to the problem of bailing out of relationships. This book is based on the precepts of cognitive behavior therapy.

Years ago I became aware of the limitations of more traditional psychoanalytical approaches toward many of the problems presented to me by my patients. At that time, Dr. Steven Fishman and I decided to open up the first center for behavior therapy in the New York area. We were slowly able to demonstrate to our psychoanalytic colleagues that we could alleviate problems such as obsessions or phobias that were not responding to the more traditional psychoanalytic approaches. As behavior therapy advanced, it became evident that not only were we alleviating these very circumscribed problems but also a wide range of problems previously presented only to traditional therapists.

What does cognitive behavior therapy offer those of you who are trapped in an unrewarding relationship? What does it offer those of you who are in danger of hanging in there and eating your hearts out until you convince yourselves that it is too late, only to have the relationship finally disintegrate in a war of attrition many debilitating years later?

Cognitive Behavior Therapy and Social Learning Theory

Cognitive behavior therapy was developed in the fifties out of a basic disaffection with long-term psychoanalytic therapy. Many dissatisfied practitioners of psychotherapy felt analytic therapy took too long and was not really relevant for helping people deal with current crises in their lives.

At the same time, there was a growth in the scientific study of psychotherapy. Before that time, there had not been an interest in assessing progress in therapy and determining what specific elements in therapy were effecting positive change. People just assumed a course of psychotherapy would make them "better," but no one had ever questioned whether this belief was, in fact, true.

Once the process of behavioral change was scientifically investigated, more and more focus was placed on the importance of the general learning theory. Learning theory became the theoretical bulwark of what was first known as behavior therapy. Later, when behavior therapy was expanded to what we now refer to as cognitive behavior therapy, the social learning theory became the general theoretical framework with which to understand motivation for thought as well as behavior.

Social learning theory simply states that the laws of learning that have shaped our behaviors can also be used to help us extinguish nonadaptive behaviors and thoughts that do not produce positive results in our lives. One example of social learning is *modeling*, the learning of a behavior by observing others engaging in it. Children learn behaviors by observing their parents. Another such law is *reinforcement*. If

feelings, thoughts, or behaviors are followed by positive reinforcement, that is, actions, statements, or any other expression
of approval, then these behaviors are learned and strength-
ened. If behaviors are followed by negative reinforcement,
that is, actions, statements, or any other expression of disapproval, then they are weakened or extinguished. These laws of
learning, therefore, help us to learn behaviors, and, by the
same token, they can help us "unlearn" or extinguish un-
wanted behaviors.

Originally, the only problems treated by behavior therapists
were phobias, addictions, and other similarly limited problems. But with new understanding of the nature of anxiety and
mood disorders, and with the addition of "cognitive interventions" in the sixties and seventies, the whole basis of behavior
therapy was broadened. Cognitive interventions involve looking at the belief systems—the life rules or mythologies people
live by—the same way we look at behaviors. Over the years,
people develop certain cognitions or belief systems through
modeling and reinforcement. That is, they learn thought patterns from models such as parents and other authority figures,
and they learn these cognitions by having "the truth" of those
thoughts continually confirmed through reinforcement. Eventually, those cognitions come to rule their lives. When those
cognitions are correct and self-enhancing, people feel good
and are happy and successful. For example, a self-enhancing
cognition might be, "My worth is based on more than just my
success at work or in my relationship. I am made up of
numerous talents, skills, and thoughts, and my performance at
my job or in my relationship is only one part of my overall
worth." When these cognitions are distorted or negative or
when they are generally incorrect—not based on accurate
data—they become "self-downing" and destructive to life.
For example, a negative cognition or belief might be "My
worth is almost totally contingent on how well I do at work or
how much people like me." Another example would be "My
worth is contingent on a successful marriage." If you behave

according to this belief, then any minor setback at work or in your relationship sets off a ripple effect that contaminates every aspect of your life, and your resulting feelings of unworthiness and anticipations of failure often become self-fulfilling prophecies.

You might be aware of the beliefs or cognitions that govern your behavior. More likely, however, these thoughts are "nonconscious," not part of your conscious awareness but not necessarily hidden away in some childhood dynamic. If you want to make a reasonable decision regarding your relationship and if you want to prevent repeating the same mistakes in future relationships, it is crucial that these negative and inaccurate cognitions be identified and supplanted by more accurate, positive beliefs that produce more constructive behavior patterns.

Cognitive behavior therapy helps you accomplish just that. It helps you to modify or change thoughts by making use of the same laws of learning with which behavior therapy changes behaviors. You can learn to model new cognitions or thoughts, you can learn to rehearse new cognitions. You can learn to extinguish cognitions and you can learn to reinforce cognitions, just as you can learn to model, rehearse, extinguish, and reinforce behaviors. With the addition of "cognitive" —thought—to "behavior"—action—the effectiveness of the entire therapeutic endeavor has been increased.

Functional Autonomy

The notion of *functional autonomy* is also important to cognitive behavior therapy. Functional autonomy refers to the fact that the environmental conditions that led you to develop certain beliefs and behaviors when you were young may have little to do with your adult life. Now that you are an adult and in a totally different life situation, those beliefs and behaviors you learned as a child may have broken away from their root cause. It is likely the beliefs and behaviors that originated in your childhood are no longer relevant. For example, if you were abused as a child, you may have developed certain survival skills, such as being nontrusting, losing yourself in a fantasy life, and being uncommunicative. When you were young, these survival skills helped you cope with the attacks, but now, as an adult, these skills are no longer relevant or appropriate to your current life situation. You may be in a relationship with a loving, caring person who doesn't understand why you are being noncommunicative and nontrusting and so on. One reason why psychoanalysis has had limited effectiveness, cognitive behavior therapists theorize, is because insights about your early life gained through psychoanalysis are usually not enough to change habitual thought and behavior patterns. Many of the problems people develop, such as unassertiveness, fears, anxieties, and so on are no longer linked to the original dynamic causes in childhood. They have taken on lives of their own. Because many people suffer from "skill deficits" (lack of effective survival strategies) or "distorted outlooks," inaccurate cognitions can only be changed through rehearsal and practice of new skills.

If someone comes to a traditional analytic psychotherapist and says, "I want to bail out of this relationship" or "I know I should probably leave, but I can't act," the therapist might do a worthwhile job in helping the patient understand why she chose this particular person and how she falls into unfulfilling or destructive relationship patterns. It is highly unlikely, however, that the analyst will be able to efficiently supply the patient with the new skills needed to bail out.

On the other hand, the cognitive behavior therapist says, "Listen, all that may be true. That childhood incident may be the root of the problem, but the current problem has broken away from the root cause. These irrational thoughts and cognitions, these self-defeating behaviors, have long since become quite independent. Tracing the cause will not help you change the beliefs and, with them, the destructive behaviors. Therefore, we have to treat the problem independently. We have to have an action plan.'' That action plan is what is missing from most other therapy programs.

This book applies the principles of cognitive behavior therapy for the first time to the universal problem of when and how to get out of a doomed relationship. This book helps you challenge the irrational belief systems and fears that paralyze you. In other words, this book helps you replace old thought and behavior patterns with more functional ones. Armed by newly acquired skills for taking better care of your needs *by yourself* and for building and maintaining good relationships, you will develop a more risk-oriented philosophy, one that allows you to peer beyond the confines of your unhappy yet ''safe'' relationship to see the wonderful world of possibilities that exists all around you.

Forever After Versus Serial Relationships

It is important for you to consider that although you may have made the vow ''until death do us part,'' many of today's psychotherapists have been discussing the validity of serial marriages or relationships. They have looked at the problem of people stuck in relationships and recognized that in many cases, people do need to move on. Basing their speculations on the notion that your needs change throughout your life as you pass through certain phases, these mental health experts theorize that it's sometimes inappropriate to hang on to the belief that you must remain effectively and happily ever after with a person you met early in your life. Yes, they acknowledge, some couples can stay together for a lifetime. This book certainly supports that commitment, but we need to point out that there is an alternative way of thinking about love relationships. More and more experts, including widely respected psychologist, Dr. Albert Ellis, suggest that pledging marital vows till death do you part may be inconsistent with modern life. The origins of this romantic notion grew from the practical considerations of economic survival. The vows that were so essential for preindustrial life are no longer relevant to the third- or fourth-generation American. In fact, many psychotherapists say, if your relationship is one of unhappiness and stagnation, the notion of lifelong fidelity to one person can be a hindrance to your development as a fully independent and realized human being. If your relationship is unhappy, the traditional idea of commitment can get you in trouble, burdening you with moral obligations that can be both difficult and inappropriate. These same experts point an accusatory finger at the popular media as the guilty perpetrators of these outmoded notions. Before the television series "Thirtysomething" and its clones, the public seems to have bought the fairy-tale notion that people somehow live happily ever after or that relationships end in a manner that conforms more to the principles of effective drama than to the gradual erosion that actually occurs in real life. Americans are media buffs, these experts warn. Americans believe what they see.

Whether or not you agree with this line of thought and decide that a lifestyle choice of serial relationships is appropriate for you, it is important to consider that you may have "outgrown" your partner, and that this is a perfectly legitimate reason to bail out of the relationship. The irrefutable fact is that staying with someone in a miserable or indifferent relationship, whether in a marriage or live-in situation, erodes your self-esteem. If your primary relationship is one of harping on real or imaginary faults, of coldness, of abuse, or a general lack of love and friendship, you inevitably come to see yourself as unlovable and unloving. Fundamental feelings of unworthiness that may have developed early in life are reinforced continually in such relationships. And the longer you stay, the worse you feel.

It is important to state here that three out of five of all

separations are initiated by women. Although *she* will be used throughout this book to refer to the reader, this book is actually designed to help *both men and women* who may have already bailed out or who are contemplating bailing out or who may be faced with the need to bail out in the future.

Self-Sabotage and Self-Help Books

This book does more than help you decide whether or not you should bail out and provide you with the strategies to guide you through the possible difficulties—real and imaginary. It also shows you where and how you can sabotage yourself and provides you with the skills to avoid this common pitfall.

The results of a study published in the June 1989 issue of the *Journal of Consulting and Clinical Psychology* showed that patients who read reputable self-help books made "improvements comparable to those that occur with psychotherapists." Nevertheless, the principal controversy concerning self-help books is that people frequently don't do the "homework." They read the book, but they really don't engage themselves in the exercises, the real meat and potatoes. Like many patients involved in therapeutic endeavors, they are passive recipients of information. They don't become action partners in change, yet these inactive readers expect change simply from reading the book. It's easy to fall into this trap of passivity because in the relationship between a reader and a book there's little sense of the accountability a patient feels toward a therapist to whom she has actually communicated about her problems. That's what makes this book different. Throughout this book we will encourage you to become an active partner in the change process. We will remind you to identify and challenge your resistances.

People have creative reasons for not getting down to the work of taking charge of their lives. Some common excuses you might offer for not doing the exercises in this and other self-help books are:

- "The exercises are not important." Somehow you are able to justify that the exercises are not relevant to your problems or to your life.
- "It's too much trouble." It's trouble enough to even think about bailing out and to read this book, you might tell yourself, let alone to do exercises. It's like being in school. Reading and thinking is enough.
- "I don't have time." You've already wasted so much time worrying about this problem that you can't afford to spend any more time on it.
- "It's too painful." You're already in so much pain, why burden yourself with any more suffering?
- "I don't want to write in this book." You're afraid if you write in it, somebody will see it.
- "I've made lists before and they don't help me." Why should this book's lists and exercises help?
- "I already know the answers to these things." You've been through this problem hundreds of times in your mind and no solution has presented itself. You already know the answer. Knowing the answers doesn't help.

Resistance to doing the exercises is often due to the fact that somewhere in your mind you know that if you do the exercise, it makes the problem real. It may have been difficult enough for you to have bought this book and to be reading it. It may seem too much of a task to actually involve yourself actively in the exercises. But the more you engage as an active partner in the helping process, the more the problem becomes real and the need for you to take some action becomes more urgent. Reading the exercise and actually *doing* the exercise is parallel to the difference between thinking about the problem and verbalizing the problem to a friend. If you don't verbalize the problem, somehow you don't have to do anything about it. If you talk about it, then you are pushed that much closer to knowing you have to do something about it. You've made it public, you've heard yourself say it aloud, and now somebody else is expecting you to act. It's the same with doing exercises in self-help books. If you write statements out in your own handwriting, then you're that much closer to taking responsibility for them. You see the "real you." You've scored a test, you've written something down, and you've answered some questions. You've now placed yourself in the process, and that can be very frightening because it means *you now have to do something about your situation.*

While you may be reluctant to take the active role this book demands, you should be encouraged to know that research demonstrates that *the more active a participant you are in the helping process, the more effective it will be.*

CHAPTER 1

Are You a Candidate for Bailing Out?

*T*he consensus of most therapists is that the couples that last the longest and who have the richest, most effective relationships generally report one primary distinction between themselves and relationships that go sour. That distinction has to do with the ability of each to accommodate the other person's differences. They acknowledge and respect those differences, are aware that nearly all couples have differences, and they accept and make those differences okay. They do not view those differences as so bad, so undermining that they have to flee from the relationship. Somehow they soothe themselves around these differences and learn to accommodate and respect them.

The following is a list of areas that if managed successfully tend to predict that a relationship as a whole will be lasting and rewarding. Read this list over and check whether you *(a)* agree, *(n)* are neutral, or *(d)* disagree.

_____ • Pride and respect
   "I generally feel a strong sense of pride and respect for my partner when he discusses his work and his ideas,

particularly in public with others. I enjoy watching him work or create. I believe he's making a real contribution to his job.''

_____ • Friendship

''I know he's my very best friend. Overall, I feel he knows me better than most. Even if we weren't together, if I had a serious problem, I would feel comfortable calling him in the middle of the night to discuss it.''

_____ • Sharing feelings

''I'm open to sharing feelings with my partner, and I sense he's willing to share with me as well. Even sexual secrets are okay to share with him.''

_____ • Bad habits

''I've learned to live with and accept as okay many of my partner's disturbing habits. Sometimes I wish he didn't have them, but I think we both realize we come from very different life experiences and our own different outlooks and habits can complement each other rather than conflict.''

_____ • Trust

''I trust my partner. I believe in his sincerity. I know he realizes how painful it would be for me if I caught him in a serious lie. Because of that concern, he won't lie to me.''

_____ • Humor

''He makes me laugh, often and sincerely. He knows where my funny bone is.''

_____ • Realistic standards

''Even though I'm concerned about the relationship, I have set realistic standards for this relationship and for my partner's behavior. In general, I accept our relationship as it is and avoid engaging in a lot of nagging because of self-dissatisfaction or other reasons that have nothing to do with him.''

_____ • Family communication

''Our family atmosphere is generally warm and caring.

Family members usually show a concern for one another. Problems are discussed as they occur. We don't seem to be grievance collectors.''

_____ • Ambivalent feelings

"I realize there will be times when I will feel very confused and disconnected about my feelings toward my partner, but I generally trust that these feelings will pass, usually to be followed by a deeper acceptance of him.''

_____ • Money

"We've worked out what feels like a reasonably fair arrangement regarding sharing and spending our money. I don't feel much resentment about money issues. I also accept that even though my partner earns less (or more) than me, it's okay.''

Rate your responses in the following manner:

1 = agree
2 = neutral
3 = disagree

Now total your score. These issues are important areas that are successfully managed by couples who do well in their relationships. Their scores would be fairly low—ten to twenty. Higher scores suggest there may be some areas in your relationship where there has not been mutual accommodation, compromise, and communication. If you don't address these issues squarely and honestly, they may continue to erode your relationship.

The following are possible strategies you might or might not have employed in your effort to strengthen your relationship further:

• Have you gone to marital or relationship counseling?
• Have you talked to friends as an opportunity to unlock some of your hidden concerns and to "reality check," that is, see if what bothers you is really that important?
• Have you set aside periods of quality time—a regular sharing period—where you and your partner sit down and

fully discuss the beefs *as well as the sources of appreciation?* Do you really listen to each other? An effective technique to employ during these times is called "nonresponse." Sit with your partner and allow him to share his concerns with you. Listen but do not respond. The idea is to avoid being defensive and to truly listen. One of the best ways to teach people to truly listen is to teach them not to respond—to avoid defensive remarks and critical comments.

• Once you have heard the complaints, have you acted assertively or affirmatively on some of the concerns your partner has raised, such as weight control, bad habits, grooming, becoming more sexually assertive? Or do you listen, register the complaints, but fail to set out a concerned plan of action?

• On the other hand, have you been able to express your complaints in a clear, noncombative manner?

• Have you read books or attended programs on relationship success? For example, a program called "Marriage Encounter" is run through community groups, churches, and synagogues. Couples get together informally for a weekend and learn various techniques, such as writing love letters to each other. There are numerous books written on saving one's marriage that contain many other helpful techniques. Have you fully explored these avenues of self-help or prescriptive kinds of resources available to you?

If you have tried these techniques and they have not been particularly helpful, and if your score is high—twenty-two to thirty—you might have already begun to consider bailing out as a viable option. The following additional exercises will help you clarify your feelings, determine if you are a candidate for bailing out, and help you begin your examination of the beliefs that rule you. Keep some paper on hand to write down your responses to the following exercises.

Clarification Exercise One

Ask yourself the following questions. How does my partner measure up to my image of the ideal partner? How much of my time and energy is taken up with wishing and *demanding* that my partner be this other person?

If you find yourself making comparisons and demanding that your partner measure up to this ideal, you are engaging in *if-only thinking,* a highly irrational thought pattern that is a prime working area in cognitive behavior therapy. Much of the misery human beings cause themselves is due to this demand that things be different than they are. If you cannot accept that your partner is the way he is and that he will never be the ideal you dream of, you suffer from the inability to say, "This is the way my partner is. This is reality. Reality is not always the way I demand it to be. It is *this* way." These demands for things to be other than how they truly are, for your partner to become an impossible ideal, are made in an *internal* language, so you may not even be aware that you feed yourself a steady diet of if-only thinking. Throughout this book your attention will be called to the irrational demands you may be making instead of accepting your reality as it is. Once you can accept your partner as he truly is along with the reality of your relationship, you can better decide whether or not you should bail out.

Clarification Exercise Two

Ask yourself the following question. What are my long-range life goals (children, successful career, world travel, etc.)?

Make a list of these goals and then ask yourself: Will staying with my partner aid me in achieving them or hold me back? Has my partner held me back? In what ways? How did I excuse it? What are the kinds of excuses I use? Has my partner helped me in achieving these goals? Is there evidence that he has helped me, or am I just rationalizing?

Look over your answers. Truly think about whether your partner has held you back from achieving your life goals. Try to determine what ways you have conspired with him to do so. How often have you said to yourself, "If I had only been married to a different person, I could have accomplished that dream?" Be careful that you are not using your partner to avoid facing your own lack of ambition or fear of failure.

Clarification Exercise Three

Ask yourself the following question. Do I spend a lot more time experiencing frustration, pain, and boredom from my relationship than I do pleasure and satisfaction?

Now is the right time to create a log of your feeling states. Keep a daily log for at least one month in which you rate the feelings you are having toward your partner. Before you start the log, look over the list of "feeling states" that follows. Predict what percentage of the time you will be experiencing any of these feeling states. After completing the log, you can match your predictions against the actual results. Be honest and be objective so that at the end of the month, the log will provide you with valuable information.

Abbreviations of Feeling States You Have Toward Your Partner

V   = Vague
Lv = Love
Lo = Lonely
J   = Joy
B   = Boredom
A   = Anger
T   = Tense
C   = Calm
I   = Indifferent
Ir = Irritation

F   = Fear
S   = Sad
Wt = Warm and tender

Fill in the abbreviations of feeling states each time you experience them under the appropiate day. Do this for at least one month.

	Week One	Week Two	Week Three	Week Four
Monday				
Tuesday				
Wednesday				
Thursday				
Friday				
Saturday				
Sunday				

Read over the chart after one week, two weeks, and one month. Look for trends. Are you angry 50 percent of the time? How much of the time are you bored? Or lonely? Are warm and tender feelings occurring with surprising frequency?

You do not want to bail out with great regrets and self-recriminations about having done so prematurely or without justification. One way to avoid this is to collect data on your feelings and thoughts. This is one of the principal techniques of assessment in cognitive behavior therapy. The log is part of the data, the evidence you must accumulate. The log is ammunition against the universal tendency to forget. Human beings often go through a relationship crisis and then forget it a few days later. You are so happy that the acute pain is over, that you put it aside. You go on, year after year, undergoing acute crises and putting them aside, forgetting. The log is a way of focusing and *remembering*. Keep in mind that your final decision must rest on accumulated evidence from this and many other exercises and insights from this book.

Clarification Exercise Four

This exercise will help you clarify and evaluate what you like and dislike about your partner. On a piece of paper list all the qualities that you like about your partner in one column. Make another column to the right and list all the qualities about your partner that you do not like. Some examples of qualities might concern matters such as grooming habits, eating habits, attitude toward spending money, spontaneous expressions of warmth, sense of humor, and behavior in social situations. Rate your reaction to the qualities you have written down in the following manner:

1 = neutral
2 = mild
3 = extreme

Now evaluate your lists and your ratings. To do this, ask yourself some questions. Which list is longer? Dislikes or likes? Which list has the highest score when you add up the ratings associated with each quality? If the dislike column is longer and has the highest score, what does that tell you?

Now look over the test again and ask yourself honestly how important the dislikes are to you. The dislike list may be longer, but do the items listed really make a difference to you? Rate the dislike list again in terms of importance in the following manner:

1 = unimportant
2 = important
3 = very important

Are these dislikes really important to you? Remember: The dislike list may be long, but by rating the importance of each item, you can consider whether or not the dislikes have a strong impact on your relationship.

Clarification Exercise Five

Here's a way to discover the rationalizations you use to keep yourself from bailing out. Complete each sentence in as many different ways as accurately describe your reasons for not bailing out:

"I am staying in this relationship because _____."
"I'm afraid to leave this relationship because _____."
"When I think about leaving, I feel _____."
"Staying in this relationship allows me to _____."
"If I end this relationship, in a few months I expect ____."
"If I end this relationship, my partner will _____."
"If I knew I wouldn't suffer if I left my partner, I would _____."

Look over your completed sentences. Ask yourself the following questions and write down your answers on a separate sheet of paper.

What do your completions tell you about your true feelings?
Are you censoring your feelings?
How do you feel when you read your completed sentences?
What surprises are there in these completions?
What are the things you've known all along?

Would you have completed these sentences the same way if you were completing them in front of your partner?

Would you have completed these sentences the same way in the beginning of your relationship?

Imagine you have been out of the relationship for six months. Do you think you would complete these sentences the same way?

Would you have completed these sentences the same way if your life depended on total honesty?

In my experience, the vast majority of patients report some level of discomfort anxiety when they think about bailing out. Look at the last sentence once more. How does your completed sentence make you feel? Does knowing you wouldn't suffer discomfort free the way for you to bail out? This fear of discomfort—the prospect of psychological pain—may stall many of you and hold you in a pattern of avoidance and procrastination. For some of you, distorted, incorrect thinking—inaccurate cognitions or belief systems—such as "I couldn't stand the pain of bailing out" maintains your fear of discomfort and may keep you from taking action.

Clarification Exercise Six

Try to determine the possible reasons why your partner may be wrong for you. Here are some sample reasons. Place a check before any that apply to your relationship. Then add as many of your own reasons to the list as you can think of.

——We don't share the same sexual needs.

——He has a different outlook on how to keep the home.

——His values concerning honesty are different.

——His long-range life goals conflict with my own.

——His notions on how to spend leisure time conflict with my own.

——He seems to be critical and undermining toward me.

Fill in your own reasons here.

_____

_____

_____

Read over your list. Rate each item in the following manner:

1 = unimportant
2 = important
3 = very important

Now rate each item again but from the perspective you had when you were first with your partner at the beginning of your relationship.

What kinds of changes do you see between the perspective you had at the beginning of the relationship and now? Has there been any change in how much importance you attach to these items? What was important in the beginning of the relationship may not be important now and vice versa. You should know whether or not you are basing your gut feelings on old values that no longer matter to you.

Carrying out several of these feeling clarification exercises will add to your ability to clearly and objectively make decisions regarding your relationship. While it might be painful or a hassle to confront these issues, it is crucial that you take on this challenge.

Married Versus Single Relationships and the Difficulties of Bailing Out

Whether you are married or single, bailing out can affect you in similar ways:

- If you bail out, you will probably feel a sense of loss. Many of us seem to believe that we need a partner to help

define us to a certain degree, to help give us a sense of worth.
- Breaking up tends to create a sense of personal failure at something you had once defined as important.
- You are losing your sexual partner, which may have an adverse effect on your sense of yourself as an attractive person. After you bail out, you may ask yourself whether or not you will ever be desirable to anyone again.
- You may be concerned with how others will feel about you and whether or not you will lose any friends when your relationship ends.
- You may have formed close ties to your partner's family. Your in-laws may not be "official," but a positive relationship may have developed, a sense of a family is to come. When you bail out, you lose that extended family.
- When you bail out you lose dreams of the future. These aspirations may differ somewhat between married and single couples, but they are dreams nonetheless about the future, about children, and about trips and projects you were going to share with your partner.
- When you bail out you lose your Saturday-night date. Losing your companion disrupts the regularity and consistency of your life.

Although some of the problems of bailing out are universal, applicable to married and single couples alike, there are certain unique aspects particular to each type of relationship.

If you are married and considering bailing out, you are more likely to have truly given up hope. If you are single, you probably still believe with a missionary zeal that you can change the situation. In my practice, I have found that the longer couples who are contemplating bailing out have been married, the more one or both partners has a sense that there really is no hope. They have gone for counseling; they've tried various strategies for communication. They've tried to patch up their waning sexual life. They may have gone to therapy as a court of last resort, but after years of abortive efforts, they really don't believe in it. They are going through the motions of trying. It's as if they want to be able to convince themselves that they gave the relationship every chance before they finally gave themselves permission to bail out. People who are single or who are living together or who are newly married are often more idealistic. In fact, sometimes they overlook or do not even recognize certain basic emotional instabilities in the other person, and they often disregard imbalances within the relationship. In contrast, the longtime couples just "know" that there are certain areas in which their partner is going to be resistant to change. They "know" their partner is stubbornly invested in particular outlooks and behaviors.

If you are single, even if you are more idealistic, that doesn't necessarily mean you are as invested emotionally in the relationship as a married person would be. In fact, if you are idealistic, you may be more in love with the *idea* of being in love than with your actual partner. In any case, you probably have less ties with your partner. You probably don't have children with your partner, so it's often easier for you to bail out. If you're married, even if you have given up hope of the relationship ever improving, there's frequently such a sense of familiarity, of investment in friends, children, and the symbols the two of you have collected over the years, that it is much more difficult for you to even *consider* bailing out. People often tell themselves that they are staying together for the sake of their children, that they don't want their children raised in a broken home. It is clear, however, that it would be better for some children to be raised by a single, relatively happy parent than by two miserable people. Staying together for the sake of the children is often a "socially accepted" excuse, which masks the fear of bailing out.

Because the marriage commitment is formal and, therefore, feels more binding, married couples tend to be more loyal to each other than are single people, living together or not. For this reason, the prospect of having a romantic relationship outside marriage may seem much more significant and immoral.

If you are married, you may view your marital vows as a formal declaration to the world that you belong to someone else, that someone wants you. Some of my patients may not value themselves, but by being married, they feel that in someone else's eyes, at least, they are a valuable commodity. To give that security up, particularly voluntarily, is difficult for many married people. If you are single, it's a bit less difficult because society, in the form of a marriage contract, has not officially validated you.

Of course, this is basically a matter of self-identity and how we define who we are. There are so few opportunities in this technological, mass-produced world to distinguish ourselves from the herd, but the one way that we can be absolutely unique is in terms of the person who loves us and who we love. However, many of us erroneously define our *total* self-worth solely on the fact that somebody else who is unique has decided to throw his lot in with us for life. If we don't have very much else in our lives to define ourselves or make us feel worthy, it is very difficult to simply give this relationship up.

The complicated and expensive legal aspects of bailing out are much more daunting if you are married than if you are not legally tied. This is particularly true if you are a *comfort junkie,* that is, if you have a low level of tolerance for any hassles in your life. A comfort junkie will begin to anticipate fearfully all of the various steps in separating and getting divorced and have a particularly difficult time taking that first step. A comfort junkie will think in terms of the entire legal, moral, and emotional morass and immediately feel overwhelmed and paralyzed to act. Rather than parceling the process out, step by step, wherein each step unto itself is manageable, a comfort junkie will believe that if she bails out, she will land in a vast quicksand of problems and pain from which she will never escape.

Static, Excuses, and Rehearsing

Once you've identified the need to bail out, it is important to move quickly rather than wait. The longer you wait from the moment of your first certain realization that you should bail out until you actually do so, the more likely you are to suffer mental and emotional demoralization and even adverse physical effects.

Sandy, a thirty-five-year-old office manager of a large industrial firm in an urban area, came to see me to report a number of apparently unrelated symptoms. She experienced difficulty concentrating, was distracted at work, and was developing certain anxiety and phobic patterns, such as a fear of heights. She also reported that she would occasionally start to cry spontaneously at home and at work. She had been married for a number of years to Gary, who she described as "lazy, depressed, boring—an uninspired husband." For the past several years, she had been thinking about bailing out. When I asked her about the kinds of thoughts she had experienced over the previous few years as these concerns about bailing out were developing, she reported that she noticed a growing obsessive envy of her co-workers—most of whom were single or "unencumbered," as she put it. They would all go out together on Friday night and have a good time, and Sandy would be envious. More and more, she found herself daydreaming about what it would be like to be single. "I just can't keep it up," she told me. "I'm always thinking about this, about getting out. It's with me all the time, when I wake up in the morning and when I go to sleep at night. Every time he procrastinates about getting a better job, I hate him."

Apparently, her husband had his own serious feelings of inadequacy and would continually put off looking for work. Gary was what is known as an *emotional bleeder*, a person who talks incessantly about his feelings of unworthiness and leans on his partner for support.

Sandy knew she was getting closer to bailing out when

Gary's innocuous little habits began to bother her. For example, she would observe him reading stories to their son in baby talk. Rather than feel a sense of endearment toward her husband, a wave of revulsion would wash over her.

Over time, I helped Sandy recognize that she did want to bail out and that a large part of her anxiety, depression, and obsessive thinking was a consequence of being thoroughly disappointed in this man who had met none of her expectations. Guilt, shame, and a sense of failure were keeping Sandy stuck in this unrewarding relationship. Our job in therapy was to help her work through the feelings that kept her from acting and to extinguish the belief systems that fueled them. The goal was to free Sandy of these imprisoning feelings and thoughts so that she could leave. To do this, we used many of the techniques presented in this book: the *five-column technique* to challenge fears, various logs and charts, visualization exercises to help inspire confidence, role-playing to learn effective assertiveness, and other strategies.

Although Sandy had a growing sense for a long time that she needed to bail out of the relationship, like many of you, it wasn't until she was able to get help in focusing on the problem and analyzing it, step by step, piece by piece, that the situation clarified. Before her work in therapy, her dilemma remained somewhat elusive to her. When she was finally able to see her situation with more objectivity and, as a result, to bail out, all Sandy's discomfort—physical, emotional, and mental—disappeared. Before she finally took that decisive step to end the relationship, however, Sandy had suffered from three afflictions that are nearly universal with people who are poised to bail out but just can't bring themselves to do it.

• **Mental static.** All people in this situation experience what we call *mental static*—a continuous background of obsessive thinking and worrying about their dissatisfaction with the relationship. These obsessive worries and thoughts were what caused Sandy's inability to concentrate, her fears and anxieties, and her bouts of crying.

• ***Excuses and rationalizations.*** People frozen on the brink of bailing out counter that mental static with abundant excuses and rationalizations about the relationship. They offer these excuses and rationalizations to friends, relatives—even to themselves. For example, Sandy kept feeding herself statements such as, "Just a little bit more therapy and he'll be better." Or "I can't be so hard on him. He's a human being just like me." Or "He's trying his best." She felt sorry for Gary and truly believed these statements. If you are like Sandy, the mental static and the excuses and rationalizations you employ to offset the static divert a great deal of your energy. It all goes toward maintaining the internal struggle over whether or not to bail out.

If you are in this situation, it's important to take a look at your rationalizations and ask if there is another way of thinking about the matter? Even if this person deserves your compassion, don't you still have the right to bail out? Aren't your rights and potential for joy independent of your concern and compassion for him? What influences are preventing you from seeing the matter clearly? In Sandy's case, her mother would frequently respond to her complaints about Gary with statements such as, "Sandy, you're being too picky." In effect, Sandy's mother was an "enabler" of the relationship. Her admonitions to her daughter helped invalidate Sandy's dissatisfaction and allowed the marriage to continue. Sandy and I had to do a good deal of role-playing in therapy, practicing how to stand up to her mother and learning to say, "Look, it may be true I have been intolerant in the past, but I have given this man ample opportunity. He is simply not meeting my needs any longer."

• ***Rehearsing.*** People poised to bail out also report that the words almost form on their mouths: "Let's stop." "Let's separate." "This is too painful." They even visualize themselves bailing out, playing out the scenario in their minds, but they just can't marshal the strength to carry it out. Sandy told me that she would lie in bed, next to her sleeping husband, fearful of waking him up, she would quietly tell him "I've got to get out." "Please forgive me, I've got to leave you." It was almost as if she were rehearsing, getting ready for the day when she would finally have the courage to really play her part. Rehearsing is a phenomenon common to many people, particularly men who have problems in expressing intimacy. As they lie next to their sleeping partners, they will repeat phrases such as: "I love you." "I need you." "You're very important to me." They are rehearsing expressions of these loving feelings in a safe setting where the person can't hear and, therefore, can't hurt them. Sandy, of course, rehearsed an opposite set of feelings.

The Illusion of the Perfect Couple

Often the need to bail out is, on the surface, not particularly clear. Your relationship may be viewed by friends and family— even by yourself—as normal, its problems typical of many couples. But what can seem ordinary to the outside world may be intolerable for one or both of the partners. The misery can be subtle, masked by a veneer of conventionality.

Diane and Don are a case in point. A strikingly handsome upper-middle-class couple married for about twenty-five years, with one daughter in college and one still at home, their marriage seemed to be successful, even ideal. But Don was hypercritical and brooding. He ruled his family with an iron fist. Whenever he was angered by his wife, Don would flare up, insult and belittle her, use foul language, claim he regretted ever marrying her, and say that she had destroyed his life. He would then go off to a room and pout, often for an entire day. When he came out and apologized, he usually gave her flowers and a gift. Although they both worked full time in positions that carried a good deal of responsibility, Diane was expected to have a meal on the table every evening and to take care of the household by herself. She would go on trips with Don whenever he demanded, even if it interfered with her plans. Don and Diane also engaged in compulsive sex because Don insisted on his conjugal rights every single night. The only times he wouldn't make love to Diane was when he was away, but he scheduled his trips when she had her period and kept track of her menstrual cycle by consulting a calendar he insisted she post on a wall in their bedroom. Very occasionally, Don and Diane would have a sexual relationship with one or two other couples. Don always engineered it and Diane went along, being typically compliant and unassertive. It was very clear that much of the focus of this man's interest was sexual and compulsive. For her part, Diane rationalized to me that she gave in to these requests because first of all, the experiences were not unenjoyable—they were, in fact, somewhat arousing to her. But beyond that, she didn't want to get Don angry. "It isn't that important," she told me, "I don't want to rock the boat."

Diane was always on tenterhooks, always careful not to set Don off. His outbursts occurred only four or five times a year, but when he did explode, she was guaranteed a day of humiliation, rage, and obscenities followed by a long period of Don sequestering himself and pouting. While Don was not an easy man to live with, there are many people who would judge Don and Diane's relationship to be fairly normal because much of the time it appeared to be smooth running. He certainly paid her a good deal of attention. But it took Diane much longer to get over his outbursts of rage and brooding than it did Don.

Diane came to see me complaining of symptoms of depression. She felt a growing sense of sadness that interfered with her work, a burgeoning sense of resentment, and she was beginning to experience bouts of spontaneous crying. What specifically prompted Diane to come for treatment was a conversation with her twenty-three-year-old daughter, who was now away at college and in a relationship. The young woman had called home and described a number of problems she was having with her boyfriend. She attributed these problems to her father's influence. "How could you stay with him?" her daughter asked Diane. "How could you put up with him?" Diane now saw the effect her husband had had on her older daughter and became extremely concerned about the impact he would have on the younger one. It was as if she had to save the younger child.

Although Don was oblivious to their problems, Diane had persuaded her husband some time ago to enter couples therapy. Things had improved for a while, but the rage and the anger soon flared up again. The message in the therapy had been "You've got to keep working at it," so Diane was shocked and frightened when our conversations finally turned to the fact that she was extremely unhappy in her marriage and that possibly she had no reason to remain. She realized that she would have to confront her fears.

Initially Diane's concern was for her children only, but after some therapy, she began to see it was herself she had to save. Like many people who are going to bail out, Diane needed to justify this great step by seeing herself as the savior of someone else. Usually the "someone else" is a child.

When there is no adult person—a lover or a very good friend—to help the bailer bridge the gap between the old relationship and a new life as a single person, a child is often used to play this role of confidante.

As therapy progressed, it became increasingly clear that Diane couldn't abide Don's rage, her constant worry about whether or not he would explode, and whether or not it would somehow mentally and emotionally damage the younger daughter. Finally, after getting support in therapy and consulting with lawyers at her firm, she waited for Don to go away and left a note. Don tried to get in touch with her. Diane insisted he go into therapy, which he did, maintaining to his therapist, "I don't know why she left me. I thought things were getting better. Why did she leave me? I gave her everything a woman could want."

But Diane remained bailed out. She arranged to get an apartment and did not give Don her address. Her daughters applauded Diane to no end; they were very proud of their mother. Gradually Don calmed down. They remained separated, and eventually Diane filed for divorce. She is now free and very happy.

Don and many others would believe that because he gave his wife sex, companionship, evenings out, intellectual compatibility, material comforts, including gifts after his big blowups, that the relationship couldn't have been all that bad. But while Don never physically abused Diane and the temper tantrums only occurred several times a year followed by abject apologies, their relationship was founded on a domination that undermined Diane's mental, emotional, and physical state. Eventually, the relationship became intolerable.

Because Diane had never given herself the option of bailing out, she had lived her life according to Don's script. When you give yourself the option of bailing out, you then have hope. Only you, the person who is unhappy within a relationship, knows the true story, and only you can judge whether or not you should leave.

CHAPTER 2

When Should You Bail Out?

*H*ow do you know when it's time to bail out? After years of treating people with this problem, I have discovered that there are certain universal indications that the time to bail out is imminent. Your decision to bail out or not to bail out cannot be based on just one particular indicator but on an accumulation of evidence—a whole series of events and problems—that add up to the decision that you must end the relationship.

Bailing-Out Sickness

Right before they are ready to bail out, many of my patients say to me, "I feel sick inside." They describe a kind of sickness they've never felt before in quite the same way, a real visceral change with genuine physiological criteria. This "sickness" differs from person to person, but the symptoms all seem to indicate that the body is telling the person to make a change in her life.

This "sickness" frequently appears as depression or anxi-

ety. Or men and women will come in to see me describing
other psychosomatic complaints. Diane Vaughan in her recent
book, *Uncoupling,* suggests that the process begins with a
secret great discontent that the initiator fastens onto. By not
being shared, the discontent becomes a very private thought,
which may cause uncomfortable feelings. Often, however, *the
uncomfortable feelings are felt before the thought,* which may
still be quite nebulous. The anxiety, depression, and physical
ailments people complain of frequently come from these unshared secrets, these unshared thoughts. Just before she bailed
out, Sandy reported feeling a kind of low-grade constant
nausea that she remembered feeling only once before, when
she was a child. Her father was being abusive toward the
family, so her mother moved Sandy and her siblings out of the
family home. Sandy described the sensation as analogous to
when you know you've eaten something that has disagreed
with you but you haven't felt the full-blown symptoms yet.
"It's like a distant sense that 'I'm going to be ill,' " she said.
"It's a two or three times in a lifetime feeling." This feeling
pushed an old button for Sandy. The sense of sickness was so
intense and so unique that she couldn't turn away from it. The
mental static she was experiencing was distracting and upset-
ting, but she could live with that. In fact, the mental static
provided a kind of escape valve for the pressure of her misery
and allowed her to remain in the relationship. She could
function with this sick feeling as well, but unlike the mental
static, she couldn't ignore or counter this gut sensation of a
vague but debilitating malaise. Her body was telling her what
her mind refused to accept. Feeling "sick" somehow forced
Sandy to acknowledge that she had to do something.

All of us experience strong feelings of dissatisfaction with
our relationships from time to time, but in a basically viable
relationship, we somehow manage these feelings, soothe ourselves, and generally work these feelings through so that they
don't reoccur. The difference between those who should remain in their relationship versus those who should use these

feelings of sickness as a cue to bail out is the reoccurrence of the feelings, their chronicity. The person who is ready to bail out experiences these feelings over and over again. Another patient, now in her mid-thirties, told me that just before she bailed out, she began to reexperience a severe pain that had been diagnosed as an incipient ulcer when she was twenty-one. At that time, she had planned to bail out of her marriage, but her husband's father suddenly died of heart failure. Unable to leave her husband at a moment of crisis, she suffered this attack and another one a few months later. As soon as she left her husband, however, she was never troubled with the problem again until fifteen years later when she found herself in another difficult relationship. As soon as she began to feel the same abdominal pains, she knew exactly what they meant. The time to bail out was overdue.

Anxiety and Depression

The most frequent symptoms that signal the time to bail out may be overdue are anxiety and depression. Anxiety can take various forms, such as tachycardia (racing heart), racing thoughts (the mind bounces from one topic to the other), sweatiness, and headaches. Depression also takes various forms, such as early morning awakening, sleep disturbances, eating changes, sad or morbid thoughts, increasing procrastination, chronic fatigue, and a general slowing down. Particular phobias may develop or they may have lain dormant for quite some time and then suddenly reassert themselves. One woman, trapped in an early marriage who felt powerless to leave, began to experience an uncontrollable fear of heights. This can work in two ways: sometimes people feel imprisoned within a relationship and develop a phobia, such as claustrophobia. In other cases, the phobia only asserts itself when they actually consider bailing out.

Panic Feelings

Both anxiety and depression often lead to the development of panic feelings, a principal complaint of those people who experience physiological symptoms. Panic feelings take the form of episodic anxiety that seems to come out of nowhere, a feeling of impending doom.

One woman who was in an unhappy marriage to a physician developed a phobia about anything medical, including blood tests, all surgery, going to the dentist, or even looking at any of her husband's medical equipment. She had been assisting him in the office and had helped put him through medical school. Now she couldn't enter the office and even had fainting spells if she passed an accident on the street. This was an obvious clue to what was going on. Sometimes the nature of the reactions are very transparent, and one does not have to be a psychologist to figure out what is happening. In other cases, such as the young woman who experienced fear of heights while trapped in an early marriage, the link of the phobia to the relationship is more subtle. Another patient reported that she was getting quite nauseous after eating and was also experiencing stomach pain. The doctors were not able to diagnose anything physiological. They labeled it a nervous stomach and prescribed stomach relaxants, but it became quite clear that most of the meals were eaten at home with her husband, from whom she felt more and more alienated. At certain times, she was able to be away from him, but at breakfast and dinnertime she felt stuck, forced to maintain a sham. The connection of her stomach problems to her relationship was tricky to spot because the problem was no longer obviously connected to her husband. That is, initially she may have experienced discomfort only after meals with her husband, but the complaint soon spread—as often happens—to all meals, thereby masking the connection to her marriage.

Secrets

Many people on the verge of bailing out begin to hold on to more and more information that they are reluctant to share with their partners. They become secretive about their thoughts, pains, hurts, even their triumphs. They do not share information about outside relationships or their disappointment in the relationship with their partner.

Ina reported that she found herself becoming more and more obsessed with holding back information from her husband. This took the form not only of holding back thoughts of wanting to end the relationship but also withholding information about what the children did in school, about her leisure-time activities, and even trivial pieces of information. It was almost as if she had made up her mind on some level to leave the relationship. She no longer had a sense of wanting to share anything more with her spouse. Even though she wasn't fully aware of it, on a gut level, she knew she would be out of her marriage soon.

Of course, the process of detachment begins before you physically detach, and one of the ways you know the process is occurring is when you begin to withhold information, often without an apparent rational reason. People often look back after they bailed out and remark to me, "It was so silly that I withheld that information." The significance lies not with the information itself but with the fact of withholding.

Reading the Warning Signs

A warning: Do not ask yourself any of these eleven questions in the heat of anger. Anger skews the results, as well as your interpretations. Ask yourself these questions several times over an extended period of emotional ups and downs.

• *Have you just stopped caring?* The person means nothing to you. You don't want to spend time with him. You're
indifferent to his victories at the job and at the bowling league.
You're equally indifferent to his setbacks and illnesses. A kind
of emotional malaise sets in, wherein you simply do not feel
as involved in this person as you used to in the past. Your
response to him is the attitudinal equivalent of "Don't bother
me with it." At this point, it might be useful to check out your
indifference. Visualize your partner having a victory (at the
job, on the tennis court, etc.) several years ago. What was
your response? Now visualize your partner having a success
today. What is your response? Compare your responses of
several years ago to those of today. Is there a difference in
your thoughts and feelings? If you become indifferent to your
partner's successes and failures, you are probably getting ready
to bail out.

Viola was married to a man who worked for the state
government. Her husband, Charles, was given a promotion
that entailed new responsibilities reserved for senior levels
within his department. He came home and told her of his
success, but she reported to me that it was like "he was
reading me a magazine article." She was absolutely devoid of
feeling in response to Charles's success. She tried to generate
some feeling because she didn't want him to know how indifferent she felt. Charles took Viola to a government party in
celebration of his promotion, and she reported that it was
"almost as if I was going through a dreamlike experience."
Viola felt disconnected, like she didn't belong there, and that
the person who did belong there was someone who could
really appreciate and enjoy her husband's victory.

Or does your partner seem to have stopped caring and
become unconcerned with your well-being? Has he always
been that way, but you never wanted to acknowledge it? The
husband of a couple I met with professionally had cheated on
his wife. Bob would assure Margaret and me every week that he
was going to try to verbalize his feelings, to let her know

when he was depressed so that she could understand why he was not relating to her. Bob's stoicism, which was modeled after his father's uncommunicative personality, manifested itself in an arrogant unwillingness to communicate his feelings. But as much as he said he would try and as much practicing as we did in the office, week after week he would make these assurances without really following through, despite Margaret's begging him to be more forthcoming. It became apparent to her that Bob did not have the capacity or desire to make a genuine effort on behalf of the relationship. He would make promises in my office, but when they got home, he said very little to soothe his wife and make her feel that he still loved her. This realization served as Margaret's cue to consider bailing out.

• *Are you experiencing a deepening sense of loneliness, of disconnection?* You may feel more alone with him than you imagine you would feel if you were actually without him. You may avoid him at home. You may feel sad when you're around him. You may feel lonely and awkward when you go out together. You may avoid introducing him to friends. You may have a growing sense of estrangement. Interests the two of you once shared may not seem to be the same anymore. That growing secret feeling of wanting to be out of the relationship may begin to impinge on everything. Sometimes you may feel as if you already live alone. This often happens to older couples who have become "empty nesters." For many years, they have been living through their children. When the children are gone, the couple's true estrangement is revealed.

One man in his sixties was living with his wife in an empty nest. Jack reported to me that for the last fifteen or twenty years, he had known on some level that when the children were out and on their own, he was going to bail out. He had just been biding his time for all those years. He called himself "a great actor," so that his wife, Rae, never guessed the estrangement he was feeling. While nothing was really wrong in the relationship, Jack felt disconnected from his wife. They had shared the job of raising their children, but other than that task, they had few interests in common. When the children did move out, he himself departed very quickly. When Jack and Rae came to see me as a couple, it was clear that he had made up his mind to bail out a long time before. His decision had come as a shock to Rae. She had not been prepared for this at all. When the truth came out, it was clear that Jack had felt long-standing disaffection and dissatisfaction. He reported that for a long time he had felt loneliness and a sense that he didn't belong with his wife.

• *Do you* **have** *to watch Johnny Carson every night?* Do you find creative excuses to avoid going to bed and sleeping next to him? Has the sexual feeling you once had for him completely disappeared? Are you just going through the motions in bed? Ironically, though, many couples report that they have extraordinary sex right before they are about to get divorced or separated. One reason for this is because they are now free. They're not angry anymore. Another reason that sex may be more impassioned at this point is that sex may have become an act of desperation. It may have become compulsive in its frequency and regularity because the sexual act is all that's holding the relationship together. Sex can be the act of two desperate people who sense the whole thing is about to blow apart.

Your sex life might offer you some clues that will indicate that you are getting ready to bail out. For example, (1) you may become nonorgasmic, (2) you may experience a sadness when you are in bed with him, or (3) you may begin to avoid variety or any requests he makes for role-playing or fantasy. Women often tell me that the sexual games they enjoyed in the past as part of their love play become annoying and disturbing as they move closer and closer to bailing out. What these women want is more warmth and tenderness. But even when that warmth and tenderness is forthcoming, they find fault with it because they are feeling a general growing sense of disenchantment.

One of my female clients had an ongoing relationship in which she enthusiastically went along with her partner's requests that she dress up and engage in fantasies with him. They enjoyed wonderful sexual variety. But as she moved closer to bailing out, she became increasingly reluctant to fulfill his requests. She felt he wasn't viewing her as a love object as much as a sex object. As she became more and more aware of his selfishness in every area of their relationship and realized that in all ways her deeper needs were not being attended to, she also recognized that the sex was all for him.

• *Do you feel abused mentally or physically?* I suggest the following rule of thumb to my female patients: If you're physically struck once by your partner, get couples therapy. If you're struck twice, separate. If you're struck three times, consider a divorce. Physical abuse does not get better unless the husband gets help. Occasionally, a man will get scared at his own loss of control and seek help on his own. More often, however, violence is an escalating pattern that will not go away just because of fear. Mental abuse, however, is more difficult to pin down and define. It can take the form of humiliation, unreasonable jealousy, public put-downs, hyper-criticism, extreme moodiness, withdrawal of affection, domination and control of the partner, and extramarital affairs.

Abuse Log

Keep a private log of when you feel mentally abused. Note how often you are abused, under exactly what circumstances, and how you feel. The abuse log is based on a technique frequently used by cognitive behavior therapists to call automatic habits of thought and behavior into awareness for the purpose of their eventual elimination. The point of this exercise is that you tend to lose track of the frequency, intensity, and duration of these incidents, and of the feeling states you experience when you are criticized or abused. You need to collect these

data over time to bring the incidences back into your awareness.
The log provides a record, or a reference point, to return to when
things calm down and you forget what was was uncomfortable.

Follow this outline to create your abuse log.

Column One: Write down a form of criticism or abuse you've
experienced. Examples of forms of criticism and abuse are:

Private put-downs
Public put-downs
Future threats ("If you don't shape up, I will . . .")
Irrational jealousy
Emotional withdrawal
Lying
Lack of compassion
Overly controlling or dominant behavior
Provocative behavior with the opposite sex

Column Two: Write down when and where this abuse or
criticism takes place.

Column Three: Write down your feelings. Some feelings you
might experience as a consequence of abuse are guilt, shame,
anger, sadness, disappointment, remorse, fear, numbness, sexual arousal, and paid attention to (ironic as it may seem,
negative attention can be preferable to no attention at all!).

Column Four: Write down your thoughts. Some thoughts you
might have as a consequence of abuse might be the following:

"I can't stand it when he does this."
"He has no right to do this."
"I better keep this private."
"I can't do anything right."

Column Five: Write down your level of belief in the justification for this abuse. Have you merited this criticism or abuse?

Column Six: How does your partner respond when you tell him
he is being abusive? Does he reject or deny responsibility?
Some ways in which your partner might reject responsibility are:

Total denial of the incident ("That never even happened!")
Minimizing the incident ("That was no big deal.")
Accusing you of being overly sensitive to shift the blame ("You're too touchy.")
Using humor to deflect blame
Telling you it was all your fault ("I wouldn't have hit you if you hadn't provoked me.")
Hiding behind a psychological explanation ("I'm sorry, but I'm under a lot of pressure.")

Some of the ways in which your partner might accept responsibility for his actions are:

Agreeing that he did it and that it was reprehensible
Apologizing
Reflecting honestly about what caused him to abuse you and how he can change this behavior
Showing later evidence of actual changes in behavior that are seen over a period of time

Read over your log. How often are you abused? In what ways? How obvious are the abuses? Do you provoke this treatment? Do your thoughts and feelings in response seem appropriate? Does your partner accept responsibility for his wrongful abuse? Most of you will have partners who use various means of rejecting responsibility, making each of these abuse interactions seem incomplete. Your log will provide evidence of abuse and remind you of what is actually going on in your relationship on a day-to-day basis. The log will help you arrive at a more reasoned decision as to whether or not you should bail out.

• *Do you feel you can't trust your partner?* You feel cheated on and lied to. So many couples come in for their separate sessions early in therapy and say, "He's lying to me, there's something wrong, there's something not right." Many women report that after cheating is discovered, they look back and recall certain personality shifts that at the time simply didn't seem very important. In retrospect, however, the changes signaled that their mates were backing off or cheating. "He stopped kissing me as often during sex." "He started using different sex techniques." It may not be about cheating, but they sense that the openness, transparency, and the "knownness" that characterized the early phase of the relationship is no longer there. One woman actually told me, after the release of the movie *Invasion of the Body Snatchers,* that "it's almost as if someone has taken over my husband. It's like a pod has taken over. It looks like him, it sounds like him, but something else is going on. There's a part of his mind and heart that I'm totally unfamiliar with right now." As it turned out, she finally had to accept the unacceptable: Her husband was having an affair, losing more and more interest in his wife and becoming more and more interested in his new lover. Do you feel your partner is closed to you, backing off? Do you sense he is not with you, and that you feel you can't count on him? Even things as unobtrusive as "He no longer talks about work when he comes home," or "He doesn't even want to argue," can be signals that your partner is withdrawing. Remember: There is always an initiator of the bailing-out process. You have a choice. You can either be passive and wait for your partner to decide whether or not he will bail out on you, thereby extending and deepening your pain and humiliation. Or you can be active. You can evaluate the situation and take action for yourself. Actively creating your destiny is always the better choice.

• *Is there an addiction or mental problem that is either untreated or not responding to treatment?* You must set up criteria to determine the probability that your partner is going to improve sufficiently to satisfy your needs in the relationship. You must understand that this is not selfish. Determining if your partner is likely to beat his mental problem or addiction is merely in your self-interest. You might say to yourself something like, "Here my partner is struggling with an emotional disorder, and I'm setting up criteria to determine if he will improve and how long it will take." It may seem a bit cold-blooded, and, in fact, you *are* taking care of yourself. Mental and addictive problems can drag on for years and years, and you need to be aware of this fact. Many of these problems do not just stop because you are being a good partner or because the person is trying. If necessary, you can speak to his therapist or addiction counselor and decide on a legitimate time limit for when he should be maintaining abstinence.

If there is a mental problem, what is the diagnosis for your partner? For example, manic-depression is far more serious than reactive depression. Schizophrenia is far more serious than anxiety reaction. If you don't understand the diagnosis, be sure to have a professional explain it to you. Even though therapists don't like to label people, diagnoses still tell you a lot.

Here are some more questions to ask yourself or a professional. Has the problem been recurrent or cyclical, expected to periodically remit and then manifest itself again over the years? What medications have been prescribed? How helpful have these been in controlling your partner's emotional symptoms? How helpful has counseling been? Are there very specific indexes of change that can be measured over time, such as frequency and intensity of anger? Is he changing?

Think about the number and frequency of panic episodes. Have they changed over time? Has the impact of these episodes on the family's functioning changed? For example, one woman's severe panic attacks made it necessary for the couple to constantly cancel appointments and affairs. This was a cause of great embarrassment to her husband.

Has the number of inappropriate social comments changed? Has the number of lost friendships diminished?

The point to these questions is to bring things down to brass tacks. You must talk about the specific dysfunctions of the relationship that are due directly to your partner's mental problems or addictive behavior.

A couple came to see me for premarital therapy a month

before they were to be married. Bonnie had just discovered that Martin had lied to her extensively about the kind of work he did. He had told her that he owned a fast-food store, but, in fact, it turned out that he was just the manager. She found out he was lying when they accidently met up with the actual owner and the subject of Martin's future came up. It became clear to Martin that the owner would inadvertently tell the truth, so he decided to confess to Bonnie at the last moment before exposure. Along with this fabrication that had been maintained for months and months were other lies about his financial condition.

This case is typical of something I often see as a therapist. I have to help the patient make a decision about whether her partner's problem is truly an ingrained part of the person's character or merely a little white lie covering up a minor insecurity. If it is part of his character, then he *needs* to lie pathologically; he needs to create fictions about himself. This character disorder is an entrenched personality disturbance that comes from deep-rooted feelings of insecurity and inadequacy. That's very different from an individual who tells an occasional lie out of embarrassment about something he did or over concern about his image. He recognizes he is lying and does it very irregularly and infrequently. A woman might lie about her age, for example, and feel guilty. Frequently, women will come to see me and confide that, yes, they have lied about their age, and that they are a year or two older than they had admitted to their partner. But when you place the lie against the entire context of the relationship, it is clear that this is not a pathological lie. It is an untruth they got stuck in a long time ago about which they feel rather guilty and embarrassed. These kinds of lies are isolated fibs that do not necessarily reflect anything bad about the person's underlying character structure. They are not part of a long trend of pathological lies that form a pattern and definitely do adversely affect a relationship.

You can often tell how troubled your partner is by asking if he feels that his lying and fabricating is a serious problem. Ask him if the lie is serious. If he answers no, then it is important to get more information about this person's values, about how he was taught principles, and how he conducts himself in other life circumstances. If this person denies the importance of the lies, then it is likely that he lies habitually. It is important for you to explore this further before you go ahead with the relationship. Here are some things to think about to help you evaluate the lying.

What is his behavior at work? Does he frequently lie to his colleagues?

When you see him with his colleagues, does he tend to exaggerate?

How much does he exaggerate and lie to friends about what he is doing, about how much money he has, about what he has accomplished?

If you are to marry and have children, what kind of model for honesty would he be?

How much does he lie to you? Count the lies.

How many of your arguments are actually about the trouble his lies cause your relationship?

Frequently, one person's lying or gross exaggerations lead to all sorts of problems for the couple. One man I saw who was a compulsive gambler constantly lied to his wife about where he spent the money he lost and about his income. He developed a chronic pathological style in his constant attempt to get money and to explain its loss.

Do your prospective partner's friends agree that he is lying? By speaking with his friends privately, you often get a real sense of how they feel about his behavior. When you aren't sure if someone is lying to you, you can begin to doubt yourself. "He can't lie this much," you may tell yourself. "What's true? What's not true? Why would he be lying like this?" you may ask. You may begin to distrust your own better instincts. Chatting with friends—his or yours—or with a therapist can provide you with a reality check, a perspective on how much he actually is fabricating.

If you are already involved with someone who continually fabricates, then you should seriously consider the option of bailing out.

In the case of Bonnie and Martin, I also wanted to find out how his parents reacted to the situation. It turned out that his mother had called Bonnie just a few days prior to the therapy session and said, "Look, Martin only told you a little white lie. It was no big deal. Why don't you just forgive him and let the wedding go on?" Her advice to her future daughter-in-law—her unwillingness to recognize the true gravity of her son's fabrications—corroborated my suspicions that Martin's lying was indeed a characterological disturbance and that his upbringing had a great deal to do with his problem. So if direct questioning is not possible or appropriate, you may decide to spend some time with your partner's parents to find out about their values.

Bonnie broke the marriage off and thanked me for opening her eyes. Before therapy, she had been ready to forgive Martin. She had felt pain and hurt, but, as is often the case, she couldn't believe this was happening to her, and she didn't want to experience another failure in her life.

• **_Do you "know" marital counseling will not help?_** *How* do you know when marital counseling isn't going to help? Of course, you can never know until you try, but if you have tried counseling for at least six months and nothing seems to be changing, you may be whipping a dead horse. You should understand, however, that according to experts, couples counseling has great variation and range.

How do you choose the right couples counselor for you and your partner? Although we often approach a professional counselor at a time of pain and simply hope that he knows what he's doing, it is important to remember that you should interview this person to be sure you are going to receive the help you want.

The following is a checklist that will help you find or evaluate a therapist.

_____ Does he start off with a comprehensive marital survey that lists your likes, your dislikes, daily schedules, differing ideas about money, children, etc., so that you, your partner, and the therapist all gain a complete idea about the way you lead your lives?

_____ Does your marital counselor give you homework? Couples need to work at home at developing improved communication skills and learning how to argue constructively. All this work cannot possibly be done only in the counselor's office. Homework can include keeping frequency counts of your partner's behavior (such as jotting down every time he engages in a bad habit). If you are engaged in trying to modify behavior, it is important that both of you recognize that there is some method of accountability. If your partner knows that you are keeping tabs on changes he is trying to make, he will probably work all the harder. Frequency counts of behaviors let both of you know whether or not the behavior has improved. If six months down the road, you are still complaining yet your partner maintains that changes have been made, the only way to prove who is right is by consulting the frequency list.

You can be told to create "caring lists," lists of things that your partner can do to make you feel loved and cared about. These lists can be posted in appropriate places in the home, so each person is constantly aware of what makes the other feel cared about and loved.

You can be told to record discussions at home that show how you interact outside the therapist's office. You can also be assigned to implement various contingency contracts—"If you do this for me, I'll do this for you."

_____ Does your therapist suggest appropriate books to you?

_____ Does he have you simulate arguments in the office so he can help you work out the issues? Only by seeing whether you argue fairly versus unfairly (such as "kitchen sink-ing" wherein you drag into the argument all past hurts and sins that may not be relevant to the present issue) can a therapist help to ameliorate the problem.

Does he actually have you role-play and rehearse new behaviors in the office? So much of what we do in relationships is the consequence of bad habits. These bad habits can only be modified through practice and feed-back. For example, does he have you practice active listening? Frequently a problem with couples is that one partner plays the "Mr. Fixit" role. One person will have a difficulty and the other will want to teach her partner how to handle it when all the troubled partner really wants is commiseration and understanding—not someone jumping in and problem solving. On the other hand, "Mr. Fixit" feels impotent and frustrated at the sight of her partner crying or being upset over a problem. Through role-playing, both behaviors can be modified.

_____ Has your therapist gone over the major areas of marital discord with you: in-laws, sex, money, children, basic values, leisure-time activities, communication skills, and how you argue?

_____ Has he uncovered any hidden agendas on the part of either partner that would undermine the success of the marital therapy? These hidden agendas can be about long-held grudges over past behavior. One wife held a grudge against her husband for an abortion he "forced" her to have years before. She refused to have any chil-dren with him because she remained so angry. Affairs and sexual secrets a partner refuses to share are other examples of hidden agendas. Does the therapist meet with you separately at least once? If he does, this should be a confidential time for the therapist to ask about things you do not want to discuss in front of your partner.

_____ What are your therapist's ideas about suggesting a trial separation if things aren't working? Is he agreeable to that option right from the beginning? Has he had any experience working with couples who are separating? Ask how specifically he helped those couples deal with the issues of separating.

_____ Is there a clear-cut agenda at each session, or do things seem to go on discontinuously? Does he take notes? Does he forget important issues? I frequently tell my clients when they leave the office to write one or two paragraphs about the theme of the session and to include a little information about what they learned and what was confusing. I ask them to bring the paragraphs to the next session. The idea is to have them evaluate the session soon after they leave. This evaluation allows me to see where I slipped up, what I missed, and where I was useful and effective. Equally important, the evaluation helps keep the couple on target. It helps them avoid losing the thread.

_____ What is the therapist's degree? Is it one of the three major mental health degrees: M.D., Ph.D., or M.S.W.? What is his training? Where was he trained? If he does not have one of these credentials, has he had extensive training in marital and couples therapy?

_____ Is your therapist boarded or certified by a group such as the American Board of Family Psychology; the American Board of Professional Psychology; the American Board of Behavioral Psychology; or the American Association for Sex Educators, Counselors, and Therapists? Is he certified or licensed within the state in which he practices?

_____ Does he have specialized training in marital or couples therapy?

_____ Has he written any professional publications or articles?

_____ What is your therapist's own personal history? Is he married? Does he have children? How self-disclosing is he? It is important to ask these questions of your therapist. A young psychotherapist with little relationship experience of his own is not qualified to do serious marital counseling.

Although it is true that many therapists refuse to talk about themselves because they theorize that revelation of their own history obstructs the therapeutic process, this notion is becoming outmoded. We in cognitive behavior therapy do not support that. We think that open disclosure of our values, beliefs, and history is very important for the success of therapy.

• *Have you met someone else?* How much are you flirting with others? How much are you fantasizing about being with other people? What kind of changes have there been in your fantasies about other people in the last few years? Is your kidding around with that guy from the office just innocent? What exactly does this transitional person or "safety net" mean to you? A *safety net,* as the term suggests, is a prospective partner who is waiting to cushion your landing after you bail out. It is essential that you define for yourself exactly what role you have given this safety net in your bailing out process. The following quiz will help you understand exactly how you have cast your safety net. What significance does he have in your life? Is this person transitional? Or is this person destined to become a meaningful partner?

Safety Net Quiz

Answer the following questions by responding (*a*) for always, (*s*) for sometimes, or (*n*) for never.

_____ Are you confiding in your safety net about your relationship and your discontents?

_____ Do you fantasize about being with him when you are having sex with your partner?

_____ Do you fantasize about a permanent relationship with this person after you break up with your partner?

____ Do you secretly or overtly become uncomfortable when
you feel that your safety net may be advocating that you
remain within the relationship?

____ Do you find that you continue to wish your partner had
many of the emotional, mental, and physical attributes of
your safety net?

Look over your responses to help you judge how significant
this person is becoming to you and if you are beginning to set
him up as your safety net in the bailing-out process.

If you answer most of the questions with "always" or
"sometimes," consciously or nonconsciously, you are probably using this person as a safety net. Ask yourself now: Can
he really be reliable in that role, or does he have too many
problems or entanglements of his own?

• *Is there a part of you that is crying out for help?* Some
people cry out for help by making suicide gestures. Jessica
was in a bad marriage and terribly in love with her boss. He
was a happily married man who would flirt with her but would
never consider becoming involved. She became increasingly
depressed and convinced herself that she could make him
much happier than his wife could. Clearly, she was casting her
boss in the role of this transitional person or safety net to help
her get out of her marriage. Eventually, she made a gesture
designed to get him to pay attention. One morning, after her
husband had gone to work, Jessica took an overdose of pills
and then called her boss. She told him she couldn't come in
because she was feeling sick. He sensed something was wrong
and called an ambulance. Jessica ended up taking a medical
leave and never returned to her job. Once she realized, through
therapy, that her feelings for her boss and her suicide gesture
were not so much genuine as her way of acting out nonconscious feelings of entrapment in her marriage, she was able to
leave her marriage and begin a life on her own.

Many people cry out for help by making subtle or obvious
overtures indiscriminately, to many men. Mary also worked in
an office setting. She was in a great deal of pain in her

relationship and became seductive not just to one person but toward a number of men. As her relationship deteriorated, she began dressing in a much more seductive fashion and flirting much more openly. She began to develop a fairly negative reputation. Therapy allowed Mary to eventually see that this behavior was actually a cry for help, a different sort of cry than Jessica's.

Still other people become less seductive when they cry out for help. They withdraw. It's almost as if they are living in fear that "If I make myself available to this person and he picks up on it, then I've really got to act. Then I've really got a dilemma."

Karen was in a physically abusive relationship. She began to fantasize about a man who was a co-worker, but instead of becoming seductive toward him, she became hostile. The more friendly and available he became, the more hostile Karen became. She was actually terrified to act because if she gave in to her fantasies and dreams about this fellow, she would probably have a relationship with him and would be thrown into conflict. A relationship with this man would force Karen to face up to the fact that she was in an abusive relationship and she would have to act on that realization. She was also terrified of her boyfriend's insane jealousy. So, for a number of reasons, she withdrew and did not act on her feelings until much later in therapy, when she was at the point that she could respond to this man and also begin the actual bailing-out process.

If you have acted on your fantasies and have begun an affair outside your relationship, you may have nonconsciously set up someone to be there for you when you take the plunge. A number of patients I have seen have done exactly this. They have set up someone up to be their safety net. They generally seek out somebody in their life who they believe will be attentive, nurturing, and solid and generally fulfill all the needs that the partner may not be fulfilling. Because setting up a safety net is an act of such dramatic change, they frequently do not acknowledge to themselves that this is what they are actually doing. It's only on probing that they will acknowledge that, yes, they've been fantasizing about someone and that, yes, that person has the potential to be a safety net when they do finally decide to bail out.

When you are setting up a safety net, you must be explicit in your thinking. You must acknowledge the truth to yourself. All parachutists try to make a soft landing when they bail out. There's nothing wrong with that, but you need to know that you are, in fact, bailing out. Finding a safety net means, in effect, that you are in the process of bailing out. When you are blind to what you are doing, you stumble along. When you have the courage to acknowledge to yourself what you are doing, then you are more effective in your actions.

• *Have you become hypercritical?* What is the difference between being hypercritical and being constructively critical? How do you make that distinction? Has the "toothpaste cap syndrome" set in? Does every little trait and habit annoy you? Has what was endearing now become exasperating?

Early on in her marriage, Betsy found her husband's baby talk during sex and romance to be very endearing. He would babble like a baby and want "Mommy" to take care of him. As the relationship went downhill and she became more and more disillusioned with him, she was progressively repelled by his baby talk and actually became nonorgasmic. She asked him to stop it. He was able to curb this behavior for a while, but then resumed the baby talk. Betsy also reported tremendous annoyance with his leaving the toilet seat up. Most women are able to accommodate that habit within the marriage, but Betsy couldn't stand it. Even his knuckle-cracking habit, which had seemed innocuous earlier in the marriage, became completely intolerable as she moved toward bailing out.

Because she felt imprisoned by the relationship and unable to free herself, Betsy focused on "the little things." She could vent her frustration on these without having to face the major problems. If she confronted her deeper disillusionments and dissatisfactions, she would have had to act. To act was a terrifying prospect. Commenting on the minor issues would not create a major catastrophe within the relationship. Commenting on major issues would, however, be quite another matter. But harping on minor complaints does set into motion a vicious circle: The more you harp on minor faults, the more estranged you become from your partner, who doesn't understand why you are becoming more and more intolerant. He either backs off himself or engages in these behaviors on purpose just to annoy you.

• *Is he always comparing you to others or are you always comparing him to others, and has that shifted over time?* Richard and Sharon were fighting so much in therapy that I began to work with them separately. What came out in the few sessions I had with each one of them was that they were comparing each other with other prospective partners. Of course, the spouse came out much the worse in these comparisons, based on intelligence, looks, sense of humor, and social ability. Both Richard and Sharon would report how their partner failed in these comparisons. Each wondered how they could have been so stupid as to think they were compatible with each other. Each was comparing the partner to a person being used as a safety net. This was clearly a case of mutual bailing out.

Very frequently, people will compare their partner to a parent. This is not unusual; even in good relationships people engage in these comparisons. It becomes a problem when the comparisons are excessive and constantly negative.

Lydia constantly compared her husband to his father. The father, a victim of the Holocaust, was extremely angry and mistrusting. Lydia accused her husband of being exactly the same. The husband, feeling guilt over his father's experiences in the concentration camp, was extremely protective of his father when Lydia told him, "I'm not going to let you treat me like your father treats your mother."

Other people will constantly measure their partner up to an

idealized parent. Rose, who grew up as daddy's overprotected little princess, shielded from confrontation, pain, and any problems the parents might have had, would constantly point out to her husband how unlike her father he was. Her husband would bring his problems home to share with his wife, and her reaction was outrage. Her daddy would never have burdened her with anything as tawdry and uncomfortable as money problems, she would exclaim. In fact, despite her anger and rejection, Rose's husband was doing the right thing in sharing these problems. Yet, because of an accumulation of disappointments throughout the relationship, Rose couldn't accept his sharing in the right spirit.

Think about your reactions to each of these eleven reasons for bailing out. Does the accumulated evidence add up to a decision to bail out? Are you, in fact, a candidate for bailing out?

Stop and think. Are you rationalizing that you are not a good candidate for bailing out? You may have decided you should bail out, but then got cold feet and decided against it. In my practice I find that my clients often rationalize themselves back into the relationship at every step of the bailing out process. They continuously doubt their decisions and question their feelings. This may be what you are doing. Look over this chapter again. It may never be more important for you to be honest with yourself than it is right now. Do you have the courage to be honest?

CHAPTER 3

How You Got in Trouble and How Screening Will Keep You Out of Trouble in the Future

*I*f you think you may be a good candidate for bailing out or even if you're still unsure, it is important that you understand how your erroneous belief systems led to behavior that got you into trouble in the first place. The more you know about yourself and the thoughts or "life rules" that consciously or nonconsciously guide your actions, the more effectively you will function in many different life situations. One reason for understanding how you got into trouble in the first place is so you will be better able to avoid repeating your mistakes in future relationships. A second reason is that if you feel reasonably sure that you will not repeat your mistakes, you are less likely to remain stuck in this relationship out of the belief that any future relationships would be just as bad. A third reason is so that you don't forget why you should stay on course should you decide to bail out of your current relationship.

Getting into Relationships for the Wrong Reasons

The right reason for entering into a relationship is that you love and respect another person enough to make a long-term commitment. However, some of you may have married or entered into relationships for the wrong reasons.

The following is a list of some common misguided reasons for marrying or entering into a relationship.

• *To get out of a destructive home environment.* Your home environment may have been overprotective or, conversely, very rejecting. The relationship seemed to be an escape from an intolerable situation.

Joanne was the victim of a very overprotective environment. Her parents couldn't do enough for her. When she was sick, they were there constantly, even when she moved out and was a career woman on her own. Every time there was a headline about a rape, they would track her down by phone. They were unrelenting in their overprotectiveness. As a reaction to her anger and resentment at this overprotection, Joanne ended up with a man who was just the opposite. Roger was mysterious, withholding, and stoic. He never inquired about where she had been or what she had done. At first glance, he was just what she needed, but, as frequently happens, she had gone to the opposite end of the continuum and was very unhappy with this relationship as well. She escaped from one intolerable situation into its equally intolerable polar opposite.

• *To have regular sex.* You may have been tired of the singles' scene and the relationship appeared to be a way out of the conflict over whether to say yes or no, as well as an escape from the threat of contracting a sexual disease. Or you may be easily sexually stimulated, but unable to say no.

Sara valued sex above everything and ended up with a man who valued it equally highly. But he didn't tell Sara that he was part of the pornographic movie scene. Although they were extremely compatible sexually, he was a shallow individual who thought of little else but sex and had never developed a truly intimate relationship. They spent their first year together in bed having a merry old time, but when the air began to clear, they discovered they had very little in common. With the help of therapy, Sara was able to bail out.

• **For status.** You wanted to be first to land a spouse or you were a victim of the time-clock mentality. You seized this opportunity because you were convinced it was your last chance.

Pamela, a fashion buyer in her late twenties, was an astute observer of her friends. She noted how bitter they were becoming at not being married. She wanted to be the first in her crowd to marry. She chose one of the first men who proposed to her, even though right from the beginning, she knew instinctively she had made an impulsive decision and that it wasn't right. She even told me, "As I walked down the aisle, I was looking for the divorce lawyers in the pews." She had convinced herself that it was better to be married and divorced than never to have been married at all. Somehow, she believed having been married would increase her future marketability.

• **Because of pregnancy.** The relationship seemed to provide the right answer to a chaotic situation.

Olga was pregnant at eighteen. She knew she was too young to marry, but her family was taking a punitive stance, insisting that she have an abortion and leave college to live at home under their supervision. Her boyfriend wanted to get married, and, at the time, it seemed the easiest solution to an impossible dilemma. Olga and her husband were completely incompatible. For the three years Olga remained married, she dreamed of little else but getting divorced and regaining her freedom.

• *Because of family pressure.* You just wanted to turn off the incessant harping of a family determined to see you "settled."

Connie's mother kept reminding her of her obligation to produce grandchildren. "I have to have grandchildren," she would insist, explaining that because of problems she had when Connie and her brother were growing up, she didn't have the opportunity to be the mother she knew she could have been. If Connie would only produce those grandchildren, her mother could finally have the opportunity to express her true maternal gifts.

This constant guilt-mongering and pressure about how Connie's chances to marry decreased every year made her feel obligated and inadequate. Finally, at age twenty-three, Connie entered into a precipitous marriage, which she later regretted.

• *For financial security.* You were tired of struggling to make ends meet and taking care of yourself. Unfortunately, men or women who are wealthy often have achieved their wealth because they have concentrated on work and have spent precious little time working on relationships. While this is a generalization and there are surely many wealthy men and women who are decent and loving, it is also true that successful individuals can be either workaholics or emotionally blocked and arrogant.

Anne married for financial security, and while she got that, she didn't really have a husband to depend on. He worked late every night and on weekends, and was never emotionally available to her.

• *To have children.* That biological clock was ticking away. You may have been victimized by the idea that one is worthless unless one has a child. If so, you might have had a child too early in the marriage, during the period when you and your partner needed time alone with each other. Or you may have wanted children so badly that you were willing to overlook problems in the relationship.

Megan was such a woman. She married and had a child

within the first year despite her sense that something was wrong in the relationship because she believed the message given her by her mother and grandmother that children are what women and marriage are all about. While she enjoyed the child to some extent, Megan discovered that she had not allowed enough time for privacy with her husband so that a real relationship could develop. The child's birth so early in the marriage was certainly a disruptive force.

• *To maintain emotional equilibrium.* You believed marriage would give you emotional stability. People who come from shaky, unstable families often believe marriage will stabilize them emotionally. I've seen this with a number of women, particularly those coming from alcoholic or other addictive homes. Frequently, in fact, the marriage does stabilize them in a way no other force on earth can, but *only if* they have made the right choice of partner. But if your choice is blind and simply reactive against your familial situation or your own sense that your life is in chaos, the marriage is doomed. Your expectations are extraordinarily high and the standards for the way the marriage should stabilize you are often impossible to meet. You imagine a wonderland with no conflicts, no fighting, and no problems.

Cynthia came from an alcoholic family. She married a teetotaler who never drank but also never had any fun. She expected her life with him would be the opposite of the emotional roller coaster she had been forced to ride with her parents. She anticipated a life of blissful calm, uninterrupted by fights. For one year, Cynthia made certain she and her husband had no fights. She was acquiescent and compliant, doing anything to keep peace in the family. Of course, she was creating an artificial environment that could not be sustained. When she and her husband began to have the inevitable fights, Cynthia fell apart and consulted me. One of the things I tried to teach her was that fighting is normal. The situation she was trying to create was a sterile one that no couple could attain. Cynthia had to learn to allow for some humanness and conflict in the relationship. Once she was able to acknowledge this, Cynthia was able to do better.

• *Because you suffer from the "fast-burn syndrome".* You are a person who loves the idea of being in love and married. For you, being in love and "merging" with someone has a poetry and drama without which your life is dull and colorless. Love and marriage provide you with a high to which you are addicted. You fall in love not with a person, but with the *idea* of love.

Like a frog leaping from lily pad to lily pad, Susan lived from emotional high to emotional high. She had no tolerance for mundane, everyday life. That was for "ordinary" people. To sustain the requisite amount of excitement in her love life, Susan would jump from man to man. At the first sign of trouble, she would leave and embark immediately on another romantic adventure, consoling her disappointment in the previous lover with the adage, "Onto the next lily pad, Susan." Eventually, the number of failed relationships mounted, and Susan came to see me. She came to discover that her intolerance of anything other than the first blush of romantic fever was due to her underlying terror of true commitment.

Do any of the above reasons for getting into a relationship ring a bell for you? Have you worked these issues out? If you have, that's wonderful. If you haven't, it may be appropriate to get some professional help. The goal of this chapter is to remind you of some of the ways you might have gotten into trouble. If these reasons are still operative for you, it would be advisable for you to seek counseling to talk about these patterns and how to develop ways of resisting them.

A woman once told me that she had been thinking about why she had married her husband. She admitted that "the needs that were met then are no longer being met now."

Ask yourself the following question: Are any of the reasons you got into the relationship in the first place no longer appropriate reasons for keeping your relationship going?

Review the needs that were met when you first got together with your partner. Do you still have those needs, and, if so, are they healthy needs? Are those needs reason enough to justify staying in the relationship? Are those needs keeping you in trouble? Or have your needs changed?

Poor Screening

Perhaps the biggest mistake you might have made was to say yes to someone you hoped was right. Because of a whole spectrum of internal and external pressures and adolescent fantasies about what your life should be like, your vision of this person might have been clouded. You might have blinded yourself to numerous clues that this person was not even "almost right." You probably didn't ask the questions you should have asked at the very beginning of the relationship or as the relationship was developing. You probably didn't make the observations you should have made of the other person. Now "Mr. Hopefully Right" has become "Mr. Definitely Wrong."

If you learn what observations to make, how to make them, and how to ask the right questions, you can clarify what you want and pass on anyone who does not fit your profile. Human beings are typically not trained to do this type of screening. Human beings usually respond with feelings, such as love and sex, in terms of what attracts us into relationships. You might become angry and defensive at being asked to think more rationally or intellectually about your choices. Some of you might object, "Listen, this is love. This is sexual attraction. This is not a process that we can intellectualize and examine objectively like scientists." This response is only a defense. Taking control over your destiny in any relationship does not throw cold water on feelings and spontaneity. As you read further you will see that effective screening—*learning to observe the kinds of traits we do not normally consciously observe*—can actually accomplish the opposite. Screening empowers you, thereby freeing you of the anxieties that inhibit loving and caring for another person. Knowing what you need and being able to evaluate—with clear eyes—your potential partner's ability to satisfy those needs liberates your emotions from the fear that comes when you feel out of control and swept away by love and lust. A number of you reading this book may not be in bad relationships, but you may gain some insights that will make your current situation even better. Those of you who are in a bad relationship now will find that learning to screen enables you to avoid repeating your mistakes the next time.

Most important, screening will help you begin to recognize your right to ask questions and check out the merchandise. You might challenge this statement by saying, "People change over the years. Screening in the beginning of the relationship wouldn't have told me how my partner was going to change." Of course, people change as relationships mature, but certain basic foundations usually remain intact. Certain basic personality traits—behaviors, values, avoidances, and preferences— are very much a part of a person throughout his life.

Do not be put off by the following list of guidelines for your screening process. Remember, everything does not have to be perfect for you to commit to a relationship. But keep in mind that most of you have been typically afraid to query, to observe, to find out who your prospective partner really is, and to define clearly for yourselves what you want and need from a relationship. It's absolutely crucial that you put your potential partner through some sort of deliberate evaluation process to discover who he is and how compatible his needs and values are with your own.

The following are some of the common reasons people use to avoid screening their partner; see which of the following match your objections:

• *"It's unfair to him."* Screening is not unfair. In fact, it may be the most fair act you can commit on behalf of both of you. If you are objective about the relationship, you can save both of you a tremendous amount of time and heartache in the future.

• *"It's deceptive, he wouldn't do it to me."* People observe and judge each other all the time, usually when they are angry or highly emotional. Their judgments are not usually made as objectively, honestly, or as fairly as yours will be during your screening process. If you are really troubled about this issue, however, you might want to consider telling your partner that you will be screening him. Tell him in a subtle way that indicates you are not just a leaf being blown passively along in the winds of this relationship.

• *"It won't help because a relationship stands on love, passion, chemistry, and other immeasurable qualities that can't be determined by questions and observations alone."* But love and passion are largely dependent on and thrive on the reciprocal sharing of good acts between a couple. When people do good things for us in a relationship, we love them more. When they stop doing good things for us, we don't love them as much. Love is actually somewhat quantifiable. People do give us goodies. They may give us goodies in terms of memories we share with them or in terms of sexual compatibilities or because they laugh at our jokes, but if you really take a look at what goes on with people, you'll see that it's a reciprocal exchange of good acts. That's why it will help to know through screening if you are, in fact, getting the goodies or not.

• *"I couldn't stand it if he failed."* Of course you could stand it. It would be uncomfortable. You would be sad and disappointed. But to tell yourself you couldn't stand it is absurd. It's far more tolerable and manageable than living your life with a man who is incompatible with you.

• *"Well, it's only one short space of time. What can I hope to learn about a person's entire life patterns?"* First of all, this is not only a brief period of your life. The habit of observation that you establish during the screening period will probably continue, albeit on a less formal basis, because you have established in yourself a new, more objective way of viewing your relationships. More important, however, is that in a relatively short period of time, you can identify some essential qualities about your partner.

How to Screen

You can screen at any stage of a relationship. It is hoped that you will begin the process of observing or querying the following areas of concern early on—before you commit—to accumulate the information you need to make a reasonable, objective judgment as to whether the relationship will succeed or fail. You may not know your prospective partner well enough or long enough to fully explore all of the following questions, but even if you can investigate only some of them, you will have more information on which to base your decision than if you had not screened at all. It is equally helpful to use the screening process now, while you are deciding whether or not to bail out of your current relationship. Screening will provide you with a detailed fund of information about your partner upon which you can make a more reasoned, objective decision. Another important reason for learning to screen now is that you will be more confident of your ability to choose more wisely in the future. Just knowing you will not leave this partner only to enter into another problem-ridden relationship—move from the proverbial frying pan into the fire—will free you to bail out of this one.

Screening Questions Regarding the Nature of Past Relationships

- What does this person share with you about his past relationships?
- How long did these relationships last?

- Were they on-again, off-again kinds of relationships?
- Were they monogamous?
- How exactly did he know that some were serious and others transitional?
- What were his criteria for a serious relationship in the past?

After seeing a man for about five or six months, Gwen discovered that her boyfriend had a number of past relationships that he considered serious. He would talk about these relationships as if they were monogamous. Because Gwen was relatively new in town and had no way of finding out anything about her boyfriend's past, she questioned him further about the nature of these relationships. She soon discovered that in every case, her boyfriend had at least one other woman on the side.

- How many relationships has your prospective partner had?
- Did he take breaks between relationships, or couldn't he stand to be alone? In other words, has he been a compulsive relationship developer?
- What made him ready for the next relationship? Was it loneliness, fear, sexual needs, guilt, or parental pressure?

Madeleine was seeing a man for a few months. During a period in which she employed the techniques we will describe as a "screening weekend," she discovered something very important about this man: He had spent very little time alone between relationships. He needed to move from one relationship to the next and described the feelings he had in between relationships as intense loneliness and desperate neediness to be with someone. He admitted that he couldn't stand to be alone. She began to notice what a clinging vine he was, how uncomfortable he felt being alone for any period of time. She realized how needy and dependent he had become on their relationship, and that he demanded an inordinate amount of nurturing.

Ideally, you want to be with someone who can allow a period to pass between relationships during which he can consolidate himself, think about what has happened, and gain an understanding of the experience. After a relationship has ended, a person needs to spend time alone, licking the wounds and engaging in personal activities. Madeleine's friend had created very little in his own life to sustain him emotionally. His life all had to do with what a woman could bring to him.

- Under what circumstances did your prospective partner's past relationships begin? It has often been said, "You marry the moment, not the woman." Do your partner's choices seem to follow that point of view?
- What attracted him to those people? Was it looks, sex, their sensitivity, their money, or just the moment?
- Were they nuturing like his mother?
- Were they ambitious, so he could relax?

One of my male clients would only date women with their own businesses so that they could bring him into their business.

- Were your prospective partner's past girlfriends passive so he could dominate?
- Did these women not want children, thereby relieving him of that responsibility?
- What kind of people was he involved with?

The point is, the more you know about his previous choices, the more you can understand about his choice of you.

Screening Questions Regarding the Ending of Past Relationships

- What circumstances exactly caused those relationships to end? Was it boredom? Was it cheating? Was it lack of compatible interests?

• What kinds of incompatibilities? Sexual, work, leisure time issues?
• Did he publicly embarrass his girlfriends, or did they ever publicly embarrass him?

Try to get a word picture of what the experience was like on a day-to-day basis so that you understand exactly what eroded his past relationships. If your relationship with him is open and honest and has gone on for a few months, he should be able to divulge that information to you now.

• How willing is he to say that the breakup of a previous relationship was his fault rather than the other person's fault?
• If he gets defensive about these questions, you need to ask why.
• What excuses is he using for not telling you about it? Is he saying things to you like, "Look, it's the past. It's over." That is not acceptable. Everyone brings a past into a present relationship, and you have the right to have at least a nodding acquaintance with what went on in that past.
• Does he pay lip service to his own responsibility, or does he really take responsibility for any negative patterns?
• If he has candidly shared his problems and admitted to you his responsibility in previous relationships, do you have evidence that he has worked on his faults since those earlier relationships?
• What kind of work is he doing to control those problems? Has he gone into therapy?

If the man is reticent to discuss past relationships, I often set up role-playing between the couple in counseling sessions in which the woman will play the part of a past girlfriend.

One patient named Alice was very concerned about her partner's refusal to take responsibility for certain problems in their relationship, particularly his pattern of lying. During screening, she discovered he had lied pathologically in the past to a former girlfriend. The past girlfriend had confronted him, and he told Alice that he had explained his behavior, but the girlfriend had been very unreasonable and had rejected him. Alice suggested role-playing. "I want to see exactly what you said to her. I want to get a good feel as to how you explained yourself and what she said," Alice told her boyfriend. After the role-playing, it was quite clear to Alice that he hadn't explained himself well at all. In fact, he had buried himself in further lies. The role-playing confirmed for Alice that it was not the previous girlfriend's problem. It was his problem.

Because all data gathered about previous relationships are based on hearsay, role-playing offers an excellent opportunity to understand your partner's past.

Screening Questions Regarding Early Parenting Experiences in a Two-Parent Household

- If your prospective partner was raised in a two-parent household, was there a lot of fighting?
- How did his parents fight? This is an important indicator of how he will fight with you.
- Did they fight fairly, negotiating differences without hurting each other, or did they constantly bring up past misdeeds, get off target and focus on other nongermaine and hurtful things?
- Were they purposely hurtful?
- Did they use their children as pawns?
- Did they "zap" each other, using put-downs and sarcasm as weapons in their battles?
- Were they stoic, bottling up their feelings, and then, all of a sudden, explode?

Dave came from a household where the parents fought a tremendous amount, and he was used as a pawn. The father was a compulsive gambler. He would sneak out of the home at all hours to get his gambling in and would frequently include his son, from age nine and up, in his secrets. "I'm going out, don't tell Mommy," he would say, often asking Dave to make up a cover story for his absence. This extraordinarily inappropriate responsibility became a heavy burden to Dave. Even when he became an adult, he was extremely uncomfortable with the idea of secrets of any kind. He could not tolerate having anything to do with the confidences of others. On occasion, his wife would confide certain secrets about her feelings and fears, and Dave just couldn't tolerate listening. He was unable to take her secrets in and protect them. Instead, he would behave in a rejecting way, either not actively listening or not commenting. Thus Dave conveyed to his wife that he didn't care about her. In therapy, we were able to trace some of this back to his early discomfort in carrying and aiding in his father's secrets. But knowledge of the past origins of the problem is not enough. As a cognitive behavior therapist, I used this information from the past for background information on the problem. Then, in addition to tracing this information back to his early discomfort, I also worked with the wife on the present, teaching her alternative ways to share secrets with Dave so that he would not feel threatened. Once his wife recognized the origin of her husband's problem, she was better able to explore other, less provocative ways to reveal her secrets. I also worked with Dave, teaching him ways to listen to his wife's secrets without becoming threatened.

- Did your prospective partner observe many promises being broken?
- Was there some sense within the family network that obligations were not being fulfilled?
- What promises were made out of convenience?

Frequently, when a child sees promises made out of convenience, he learns to do the same thing. He will make promises he does not intend to keep out of convenience, just to "get the old lady off my back."

Darryl was raised in an environment in which his father would frequently make all sorts of promises to his mother just to stop her nagging. Darryl even described to me how his father would make a promise and then wink to Darryl, as if to say, "Hey, promises are worthless." Of course, this behavior was modeled by Darryl and became a serious problem in his relationships. His broken promises were around typical issues, such as money and leisure time, and behavior, such as gambling, drinking, and other women. Karen, Darryl's partner, was concerned because Darryl was continually making these types of promises and failing to keep them. Darryl knew on some level that his behavior was wrong, but it was observed and reinforced so strongly over so many years that it was almost uncontrollable. In the beginning, he even felt his behavior was justified.

- Which of your prospective partner's parents was dominant? How was that dominant-submissive pattern manifested? What did he learn about who wears the pants in the family?
- Did he learn women are to be respected or that they are servants? Or was his father henpecked and dominated?
- What did he model from his parents about appropriate roles for men and women?

Alan was raised by a mother who was a feminist zealot. As described by Alan, his father was a wimpy, frightened fellow who went along with the mother's beliefs and behavior to the point that she was actually cruel to her husband, humiliating him in front of her female friends and making him the butt of jokes. In a case such as this, the son could go in either of two directions: He could choose a woman like his mother or take the opposite tack and select a passive, ultrafeminine, submissive kind of partner. Alan, in fact, was trying to make up his mind. He was terrified that he would become involved with a woman like his mother. His fear had led him into a relationship in which the only criterion for his partner's behavior was that she not act in any way whatsoever like his mother. Whenever his partner seemed to be behaving like his mother, Alan would react in an overly dramatic and totally inappropriate manner.

Another important issue is what messages your prospective partner's parents communicated about marriage. Comments such as "What a mistake I made," "Listen to me, don't ever get married," do not fall on deaf ears. One woman patient I saw told me that her mother would constantly repeat to her, "Don't make the mistake I made. Marry for money. Don't marry for love." Another client of mine whose father was a failed businessman was continually advised by her mother, "Marry a professional man," and, of course, that message had the opposite effect. The daughter grew up with a penchant for struggling artists or working-class men.

Whether parental messages have an opposite or reinforcing effect is often based on the amount of trust and respect that the person has for the conveyer of the information. Find out what he observed in terms of his own parents' experience.

Screening Questions Regarding Early Parenting Experiences in a Single-Parent Household

Judith Wallerstein's research on single-parent families emphasizes the absolute importance of shared responsibilities for the child's upbringing after the separation, and the potential negative impact on children when parents are at war with each other. If they are cooperating and the child senses that spirit of connectedness on his behalf, he will do better. If your partner comes from a single-parent home, you want to get a sense of the extent to which the noncustodial parent was involved in your partner's childhood.

- What was the nature of the relationship with the noncustodial parent?
- Was that absent parent constantly put down by the custodial parent or was there a sense that both parents cooper-

ated and negotiated important decisions in raising their child?
- What was the quality time like with each parent? Were there rushed weekends and long afternoons alone after school? As a result, how does your partner now define quality time with a parent?

When Paul was six years old, his mother was institutionalized for manic-depression. He was raised by his heartbroken father in a strongly bonded all-male environment that included a brother and some uncles. Paul grew up with very uncomfortable feelings about women that were modeled after his mother's eccentric behavior: He believed that women were unpredictable, would often behave in bizarre ways, were untrustworthy, and were heartbreakers. Of course, these beliefs manifested themselves in his marriage. Paul was extraordinarily jealous of his wife's behavior, almost to the point of paranoia. He didn't trust her to go out alone, and he kept close tabs on her every moment.

- If your prospective partner was raised by either his mother or father alone, what was that parent's relationship with the opposite sex?
- Was the parent mistrusting, oppositional, hostile, needy, desperate, or protective of the child?
- What explanation was given to your prospective partner about the single parent's dating activities? How did he accept it?

Children of divorced parents who live with the mother or the father often resent the people their parents date. The child may believe that the mother or father is abandoning her for a new partner and that the parent has made a terrible mistake in getting rid of her spouse. Children with this experience may grow up resenting or fearing new situations or new people that come into their lives. Others may become very needy or jealous in relationships and are terrified to let go.

Screening Questions Regarding Coping with Family or Parental Problems

- Was mental illness or addiction part of your prospective partner's background?
- If so, how did the parents cope with these problems?

For example, there has been tremendous activity in the past few years on behalf of adult children of alcoholics. Information is now plentiful and they even have their own self-help groups. These people grew up in highly unpredictable environments. They never knew what mommy and/or daddy would do, so they developed a lack of trust and a sense of insecurity in their adult relationships.

- How were problems of mental illness or addiction handled and presented?
- Was your prospective partner encouraged as a child to believe that this wasn't going to happen to him?
- Or was the mental illness sometimes used as a punitive measure?

One male patient was told by his mother that if he didn't shape up in school, he would end up just like his father, who was in a mental hospital. This man grew into adulthood with this fearful prospect looming over him to the point that whenever he had any anxiety, he was convinced he was going to go crazy. Needless to say, the effect on his relationships was deleterious. He was constantly asking for reassurance and running to doctors with hypochondriacal complaints. Few women could tolerate his behavior.

Try to determine if, in general, there was a conspiracy of silence in your prospective partner's childhood home about the family's problems or if they were discussed openly and honestly, with brainstorming included in the discussion, to generate alternative solutions. Was the child involved in that process? The key here is to discover how problems were handled within the family. What problem-solving styles were modeled when working out difficulties within the family?

When I was growing up, we had a "Sunday Breakfast Club." Every Sunday, my parents would call me downstairs to sit around the table and have a meeting. We would vote on family issues: Do we buy a pool table? Do I go to religious school? When a crisis erupted in the family, we called a special meeting. The votes were always stacked, of course, but a kind of democratic atmosphere evolved. I had a sense that I had a say in family matters. It was so interesting to me that every week I put together a little newspaper, *The Lubetkin Gazette,* and sold it to my parents for one cent.

It is important to have an understanding of what the atmosphere in your partner's home was like and how problems were solved. What he modeled in his parental home defines in large measure what he will bring to your relationship. The familial sense of democracy will become intergenerational. A man who is brought up in such an environment will most likely help create the same atmosphere in his relationship with you and your children. For example, the same democracy exists today in my home with my children. Of course, inflation has raised the price of *The Lubetkin Gazette* to five cents.

Screening Questions Regarding Gifts

What gifts does your prospective partner give for birthdays and other special occasions? The kinds of gifts a person gives are extremely important in telling you about him. Does he give a gift certificate? That's very different than giving roses. Giving roses is very different from giving a humidifier. Note what kinds of gifts he gives you. Also evaluate the kinds of gifts he gives to his parents, sisters, brothers, and friends.

One woman constantly complained about her boyfriend who always gave her gift certificates. His father had always given his mother gift certificates, so he could never understand why she was so upset. His rationalization was, "Whatever I get her, she doesn't like." He missed the point that even if she didn't like anything he got her, what mattered was the act of giving, the fact that he went to a store and spent time and effort to pick something out for her. It took a great deal of time and work to get this man to recognize the distinction.

One man always gave his wife appliances for her birthday. One time she sent him to Fortunoff's, specifically the jewelry department, thinking she was completely safe and that he would have to buy her jewelry. But his image of his wife as a domestic goddess remained intact; he bought her a silver-plated crumb duster!

Ask yourself if your partner gives gifts designed more for his own enjoyment than for yours. Frequently, a man will give a gift he will enjoy rather than one chosen for the recipient, for example, he might buy tickets to a show *he's* been wanting to see or even to a sporting event in which the recipient is totally uninterested. The ingenious rationalization might be something along the lines of "Well, I want her to learn more about basketball, and this is a perfect opportunity for us to share that interest."

Does he give image-oriented gifts? Or is the gift designed to impress rather than to meet your real needs? These differences may be subtle, but they are nevertheless important. One client wanted a particular piece of jewelry. Her boyfriend insisted on taking her to a famous, status-heavy store despite her insistence to shop in a jewelry district where he could purchase the same piece for substantially less. He kept saying, "Honey, you're worth more than that." At first glance, this seems very loving on his part, a sign that he's really committed and concerned about her. But the issue was not that simple. This man was very image conscious and felt uncomfortable about buying the jewelry any other way than the status route. He ended up spending twice as much for the piece. His girlfriend was uncomfortable about the amount he spent and did not enjoy wearing the jewelry. In fact, he hadn't listened to *her* needs and what *she* wanted. He had insisted on doing it his way.

Does your partner ruin surprises? Another common problem is that some men will ask what their partners want, thereby ruining the surprise. They justify this by saying, "If I don't ask, how will I know what she wants?" But many women don't want to be asked. They want to be surprised. Again, it's the problem of the man's sense of practicality versus the woman's need for emotional generosity.

Does your partner give gifts late, long after you've been disappointed? I have a good friend who constantly gave gifts after the fact, never on the day of the birthday or the anniversary. This behavior indicated resistance concerning the relationship. But he never talked about his pain. He just acted it out by giving gifts late.

Screening Questions Regarding Your Partner's Friends

- What kinds of friends does your prospective partner have?
- How healthy are those relationships?
- Does he have friends of the opposite sex? If so, how do you feel about this?
- Does he choose friends who are compliant or complementary, or with whom he's competitive?
- What kinds of people does he attract?
- Are there ego boosters, narcissists, or lowlifes among his crowd?
- What opinions do his friends have about women?
- What are their opinions about marriage?
- How influenced is he by them?
- What are their habits?
- How do they spend their leisure time?
- What are their values?
- Are they likely to become problems for you as a couple in the future?
- Is he unreasonably bonded to them?

- Does he insist on having his regular night out with the guys even if it interferes with some activity you need to be doing as a couple?

I am currently seeing a male patient who is a sports nut and engages in sports activities with his buddies at least three nights a week. He is absolutely unwilling to alter that schedule in any way. Because his work often requires him to work late, his wife is usually stuck at home alone with a toddler, missing him. Of course, these frequent nights out are masking the fact that he is unhappy in the relationship for a number of reasons. He holds on to this outdated teenage commitment to "the boys" for dear life, because if he lets it go, he will have to spend unstructured time at home at night alone with his wife. In therapy, we are working to overcome his resistance to spending consistent quality time with his wife. They need this time so they can voice appreciations of each other and share and solve problems together.

Screening Questions Regarding Quality Time

- How much quality time does this person spend with you?
- How willing is this person to give up his work schedule for a friend or family member in a crisis?
- How did he respond the last time there was a crisis?

Over and over again I see that people will tend to bail out or not be available when there are crises such as a death or illness in their partner's family or if that partner suffers a protracted illness.

If there have been no crises during the time of your relationship, ask your partner if there have been similar crises in his life or in a previous partner's life in the past, and, if so, what happened? For example, in my own relationship, whenever my wife would feel a little sad or depressed and want to stay in bed for part of a day, I would get enormously angry and restless. We consulted a marriage counselor for a few sessions

to discover what was going on. The counselor reminded me
that when I was fifteen years old, my mother had died of
cancer. She had spent the last year of her life in bed, sick and
depressed. When he prodded that memory, a light bulb went
on in my head. Of course, I was having these powerful
reactions. That was a button being pressed about which I was
unaware. Once I had that information, I was able to replace
that old belief system with more appropriate cognitions and to
"rehearse" new behaviors in response to my wife's need to
stay in bed.

Screening Questions Regarding Assumption of Personal Responsibility

How willing is this person to admit to a mistake? Ask yourself
if you have ever heard this person say, "I'm sorry." Being
able to admit to one's mistakes is terribly important. Can he
acknowledge he has made a mistake, that he is at fault to some
degree in the situation, or can he at least say to you, "I'm
sorry if what I did hurt you or upset you. That was not my
intention." That is a key phrase many people cannot utter and
need to learn to say. While it is not a full acknowledgment
that he was at fault, it is an acknowledgment that if he hurt
you, he apologizes and assures you that the hurt was uninten-
tional. In counseling, we often have couples reverse roles and
argue the other person's position. You can try this on your
own. If you have told your partner that he hurt you and he
professes complete inability to understand how he could have
hurt you, then reverse roles. Your partner will take your role
and try to feel what you are feeling. This exercise helps to
teach empathy, the ability to identify what it feels like to be
the other person in that particular situation. It also helps your
partner identify his resistance to saying, "I'm sorry." Men
frequently have all sorts of resistances to apologizing: "It's
wimpy." "It means I'll lose face." "My father never did it

for my mother, so why should I?'' ''I'm afraid if I apologize, she'll begin to take advantage of me the way my mother took advantage of my father.''

Screening Questions Regarding Children

- How does he behave with children?
- Does he become impatient?
- Can he get on their level and be silly with them?

I will never forget a couple I saw years ago. The wife came in, ready to bail out. She complained that her husband was never able to relax with their children. As it turned out, this man had never learned how to be playful and spontaneous. We spent hours on the floor in my office, rolling a ball back and forth, conversing in nonsense talk. The couple's children came in a few times and joined their father and me on the floor. I literally had to train this man in how to relax all of his inhibitions to become spontaneous and silly.

Screening Questions Regarding Pets

How does he behave with pets? If your partner is kind to pets or takes a liking to your pets, that *may* be a statement about how he is going to be with children or a measure of how comfortable he is with your symbols, the things that are important to you. It may be a way of deciding how generous he is.

On the other hand, many people are very comfortable with safe, nondemanding beings. They freeze when it comes to giving love to a person, someone to whom they will feel an obligation or who is going to require more than a pet.

Screening Questions Regarding Humor

- Does he have a good sense of humor?
- Is it compatible with yours?

There are different types of humor. Obviously it's best if the two of you can laugh at the same kinds of things. Some couples I have seen went to comedy clubs and disagreed violently about the humor. This ended up causing some concern about the relationship. "How come we laugh at two completely different kinds of humor?" The main incompatibility usually is around dirty jokes versus nondirty jokes. Unfortunately, most people will laugh at put-downs and sarcasm. On the other hand, many people do not laugh at dirty jokes. They become embarrassed or offended. Another common difference is that one person doesn't appreciate the wry, cutting humor of the other.

- Does your prospective partner have a sense of irony, of the absurd?
- Is he able to laugh at himself?
- Does he always take life seriously?

Those are central questions, particularly when a couple is having differences. When you and your partner are arguing, you need to take a break and look at how you're arguing with each other. One of the things I encourage couples to do when we simulate arguments in my office is to step back about halfway through the dispute and recognize the absurdity of what's happening and to notice how they are becoming stuck unreasonably in their respective points of view. At these halfway points, it's good to try to find something light or humorous about what's going on. If your partner seems incapable of doing this, if he is deadly serious about everything, it augurs badly for your relationship.

It is equally important that your partner be able to laugh at himself, at his personal failures. Some men come home with problems or failures at work that they take so seriously that it creates a pall over the family for days on end. At some point, these men need to be able to stand back from the situation and laugh about it a little bit.

Truly dangerous humor is humor that is sarcastic or puts people down. If your partner is a joke teller, what kinds of jokes does he relate? Are they mean-spirited or prejudicial? This tells you a good deal about the kinds of ideas he values and the kinds of things he finds humorous. The classic example is the man who hurtfully airs in public funny but humiliating stories involving his wife. He loves to relate stories that are really hurtful about her bonehead mistakes in situations such as adding up a bill incorrectly or talking to the children's teachers. The story may get a laugh but the joke is at his wife's expense.

Screening Questions Regarding Sharing of Feelings

- Is he willing to discuss his personal feelings, dreams, failures, and confusions?

Look for the "I feel's" rather than the "I think's" in his comments. Is he able to talk about what he really feels inside rather than intellectualize his feelings away?

- Can he acknowledge confusions and uncertainties easily?
- Does he take responsibility for his failures or does he blame others?
- Is he so perfectionistic that he can't accept his own mistakes?

The key question is Can he acknowledge his own personal dilemmas in life? Can he talk about them or doesn't he share his dreams, aspirations, fears, and anxieties about repeating past failures?

A very stoic fellow was married to an actress. Her work and training had brought her close to her feelings. She was able to pull them up, feel them, and look at them. She would ask her husband how he *felt* about a situation involving their daughter, and he would answer with a *thought*. She would ask him how he saw himself within their family, and he would respond with an answer totally focused on his work or a promotion he was gunning for. She would ask him about confusions and uncertainties he might be feeling, and he would deny any such feelings and act as if everything was clear and well formulated. She shared with him her failures in her career, hoping that would prompt him to talk about his own, but he would always come across in the most optimistic terms, never allowing any doubts.

One day, he was fired. He was devastated, not only because he was fired, but also because he had never learned how to mourn this kind of loss or how to talk openly about his feelings. This event spelled disaster for the relationship. He began to spend weeks in bed without ever acknowledging to his wife that he was feeling depressed. He kept saying, "I'm thinking. I'm thinking things through." Because he had never learned the skills of acknowledging painful feelings and talking about them and felt extremely embarrassed, he withdrew. He became clinically depressed and had to go on antidepressant medication.

When looking over your reactions to these screening items, keep in mind that no relationship stands or falls on any one or even several of them. What you are looking for is an accrual of evidence. Your decision on whether or not to bail out will, of necessity, be a partly subjective one. You can't legislate how many items your partner has to fall short on before you should bail out. These areas of concern are really a prompt, a suggestion as to what elements are important, the ones that tend to make or break a relationship. Some relationships survive well with several missing; others can't survive unless almost all the elements are intact. What is helpful, however, is to use these areas of concern as a guide in your concentrated, purposeful effort to decide whether or not a partner is suitable for you.

This effect has been formalized in an exercise called the "screening weekend."

The Screening Weekend

You have been seeing someone and the time has come for you to decide whether or not you want to make a commitment. The *screening weekend* is a period of time you set aside for purposeful observation and questioning of your prospective partner on the above areas of concern. This screening weekend can take place over any length of time you find appropriate. Your prospective partner doesn't have to know that you are observing him, but on this weekend, you will be a kind of scientist. You will learn to be more objective. You will not allow your "gut feelings" to lead you, because they could take you to what could only be a short-term satisfaction. In the long run, you could end up miserable. If you are already miserable in your current relationship, a concentrated period of "scientific" screening will help you identify the causes of your misery, and, as we have stressed earlier in this chapter, screening will provide you with the information you need to make a reasoned decision on whether or not you should bail out.

First, look at how you are objecting to this suggestion. What are some of your excuses? You might be saying to yourself, "A relationship should be spontaneous, not scientific." "Love can help me change him." "I'm not a shrink; I won't know what to look for."

Those are only rationalizations you make to yourself to avoid the possibility that you might have to confront information that may force you to break off the relationship. Many of us spend many hours, even days, researching financial plans, deciding on which school to send our child to, evaluating where to get our hair cut, and studying the pros and cons of other decisions in our lives, yet we are often reluctant to apply the same careful research toward a love relationship. We prefer to go by a "feeling," discarding all we know about good, objective fact-finding.

Perhaps, though, these suggestions on screening will add something to your storehouse of knowledge and help you realize that some sort of screening process is essential. If you realize that you may not have screened well in the past, screening in the future, after you bail out, will help you to make that necessary break with your past patterns—the less-aware belief systems and the resultant behaviors that got you in trouble. Knowing you are able to screen better in the future will reassure you that you won't go through the ordeal of bailing out of one relationship only to land in another relationship that is a carbon copy of the earlier one.

You may think screening is silly. You may think it's cold-blooded, but try it. You may be surprised at what you learn.

Rules for a Screening Weekend

1. It doesn't have to be a weekend. We call it a weekend to encourage you to set aside a specific time to look at some of the issues listed earlier in this chapter. The weekend can, in fact, be a week or it can take place on several different occasions. The point is to have enough time to thoroughly observe a number of key concerns.

2. Sample your partner's behavior in a wide variety of circumstances and answer as many of the key questions as you can, either by direct questioning or by observation.

3. You are not looking for a 100 percent perfect performance on his part. You are merely looking to collect information and to compile evidence that leans one way or the other.

4. You must try to be as objective as possible in your evaluations. Try to see what's *really* going on, not what you are *afraid* or *hope* is going on or, out of anger, what you *suspect* is going on.

5. You must resist showing great disappointment or joy at his responses. You don't want to tamper with your collection of information by swaying his behavior through your emotional reactions.

6. You must document your observations. The following is a guide to setting up a chart that will help you document the information you gather in such a way that you can more easily evaluate it.

To document the results of your screening weekend, record your observations on a large piece of paper or oaktag using the following outline.

Column One: List key issues or concerns.

- Past relationships
- Parental influence
- Gifts and generosity
- His friends
- Quality time
- Admission of mistakes
- Children
- Pets
- Sense of humor
- Admission of feelings

Column Two: List your questions directly to the right of each key concern.

Column Three: List his answers in the column directly to the right of column two.

Column Four: List your observations in a column directly to the right of column three.

Column Five: Rate your satisfaction score in the last column. This score measures your satisfaction with your prospective partner's answer to each question or with your observation of his behavior regarding each key concern or issue. Use the scoring system on the following page.

1 = poor
2 = fair
3 = good
4 = great

Be aware that in many circumstances your gathering of information on the issues will not be gained by direct questioning of your partner. Your information will often be based solely on your observations. This chart will help train you to become a better observer than you have been in the past.

The following is the story of one woman's screening weekend. Amanda came to me feeling a low-level anxiety about her relationship. She wasn't sure what the problem was although she had isolated a few areas of incompatibility. She felt the relationship as a whole was valuable and wanted an objective sounding board.

Therapy is often another kind of screening. The client bounces ideas she's already formulated off someone else, in this case, the therapist. Amanda talked about her partner's lack of a sense of humor and generosity and a few other issues. We set up a screening chart and she screened her partner over two weekends during which they spent time together almost exclusively at his summer vacation house. Amanda was afraid the screening would short circuit her passion, but she discovered, interestingly enough, that being observant and vigilant didn't interfere with her romantic feelings at all. If anything her feelings of being in control for the first time—collecting information that she would be able to sort out with me later—enhanced her ability to be freely romantic.

Essentially, Amanda found that her partner was acceptable in some areas, such as past relationships and parental modeling. She was somewhat concerned, though, about his generosity because he had not suggested paying for her travel expenses to the summer house even though he could well afford to do so. He also failed to meet her at the ferry landing to accompany her to his house even though she had hurt her leg a few weeks earlier and was still somewhat injured. In addition, while lying out under the stars on the beach, she realized that he was not able to talk openly about what he was feeling. For Amanda, it was a very romantic, impassioned time, but he couldn't find words. She needed him to verbalize his feelings and his experience of their special time together. When a few of his friends came by, she was very turned off. They were adolescent, beer-guzzling, and disruptive; furthermore, they made pejorative remarks about women. Finally, some children who lived nearby started playing in front of the house, and he was very brusque with them. When she asked him about how he felt about the children, he just called them "brats."

After we processed her screening results two times, Amanda decided this man wasn't for her, and she bailed out. She reported that the screening process had objectified and clarified the situation and made her decision easier. When Amanda had first come to see me, her feelings and thoughts were a morass. Screening helped her to distance herself from these thoughts and feelings, to determine what was really going on, to identify what exactly she wanted in a partner, and, therefore, to make a good decision.

CHAPTER 4

Why You Stay in Trouble

*T*here are several possible reasons why you may have stayed in a troubled relationship. You could be a "love slob." Or you could be "risk adverse." You may live with the fantasy that it will all change because you are operating under the rules of a "hidden bargain." You may have "low frustration tolerance," or you could suffer from "discomfort anxiety." These terms all refer to patterns of behavior that may have been learned by modeling your parents' behavior or may have developed over many years within this or other troubled relationships. These patterns of behavior are frequently related to issues involving self-esteem, that is, how or why you value yourself.

Are You a Love Slob?

Are you a victim of what internationally known psychologist Albert Ellis calls the "love-slob syndrome"? The love slob cannot stand the idea of being alone, and that's what keeps her stuck in a relationship. If you are a love slob, you obsess

about your love object, and you convince yourself you can't
survive without him. You experience actual physiological and
psychological withdrawal symptoms when you are separate.
To help determine whether or not you are a love slob, take this
test. Rate your answers to the questions below by using the
following scale:

1 = strongly disagree
2 = disagree
3 = neutral
4 = agree
5 = strongly agree

_____ Without romantic love in my life, I feel like a nothing.
_____ It is very important to me that others know I am in a
relationship.
_____ A bad relationship is better than none at all.
_____ The idea of being alone without a partner terrifies me.
_____ When I am in love, I lose interest in my friends.
_____ I would gladly give up the chance to go to a favorite
activity if my partner summons me at the last moment.
_____ I truly believe that being loved makes me a more worthy
person.
_____ When I think I'm going to break up with my partner, the
feelings are horrible and overwhelming.
_____ I often find myself feeling very insecure that my partner
will stop loving me.
_____ I *couldn't stand* the knowledge that my partner loves
someone else as much as me.

If you score from thirty to fifty, love may define your self-
worth far more than it legitimately should and being in a
relationship may be the most important aspect of your life.
Without a relationship, you feel diminished in value.

Love slobs lose perspective while they are in the relationship. This loss of perspective is generally expressed in two
ways: They have a tendency to become overly compliant,
overly nurturing, overly jealous, and overly desperate; and

they tend to become emotionally devastated when the relationship goes sour.

If love slobism is one of the reasons why you are remaining in an unsatisfactory relationship, you should try to combat this syndrome. Let's first look at why you are a love slob.

Love slobs tend to define themselves almost totally in terms of another person's approval and acknowledgment. If this is true for you, you may suffer from what therapists call "contingent self-acceptance." For example, if you are a woman, you may have come from a home where your mother was your father's "slave," capitulating constantly to all your father's whims. Or your father may have withdrawn from your mother and the children. In such a situation, you learn either that your own needs are simply unimportant or that they are less worthwhile compared to a man's. What you infer and come to believe is that you are worthless unless you can win the love, attention, and aprroval of a man.

Gwen's father was extremely passive on the surface, but, in fact, his compliance masked extreme hostility. He allowed his wife to take over in the relationship. Essentially, she raised the children alone, meting out both discipline and love. Gwen's father would always use work as an excuse, but basically, he was emotionally withdrawn, never engaging with either his wife or his children. He would sit in front of the television set for hours and hours, occasionally grunting approval or disdain. Essentially, he was an invisible presence, so much so that when I asked Gwen to visualize her father, who had died a few years before, she had a difficult time even conjuring up an image of his face.

Gwen "desperately" needed someone to love her, a male figure to fill the emotional void her father never filled. As soon as any man began to pay attention to Gwen, she immediately lost all perspective and became desperate, losing herself in the man and defining her whole being by whether or not he attended to her. She would shower him with gifts, call him frequently and at inappropriate times. She would send her spies out to check on what he was doing and who he was with. She had no sense of the appropriate slow and gradual development of a relationship. Of course, her behavior typically turned her love object off. Gwen consulted with me because the man she was seeing seemed more and more distant although he was perfectly happy to take her gifts. Gwen couldn't understand why her "love" wasn't being returned, and she seemed impervious to his unfair treatment. Ironically, love slobs such as Gwen hang in there despite the cold treatment they invariably receive, and then, after a long period of pain and humiliation, they nearly always lose their love objects.

Another reason why you may remain stuck in a troubled relationship is that you may be overly concerned about your public image, that is, whether or not other people see you as part of a couple. This may cause you to suffer great discomfort if you find yourself without a love relationship. Because you define yourself almost entirely in terms of your relationship, it doesn't matter if that partner values you and cares about you. All your concern is wrapped up in your public image. Furthermore, you may typically undervalue yourself unless other people know you have the attention of a "prize" man; just a nice man won't do.

Lydia was overly concerned about how others viewed her relationships. Because she valued her public image even more than the self-esteem she gained from the relationship itself, she would tend to choose men who were very good looking, successful, and sophisticated. She would make certain to be seen by everyone she knew when she was out with such a man. Once, when she was seeing a wealthy man who traveled by limousine, she had him drive by her friends' homes and invite them down to join her and her date for a drink in the limo. On the surface, the gesture seemed like simple friendship, but in therapy, Lydia owned up to the fact that it was very important to her that her friends see the kind of catch she could land. In actuality, the man offered Lydia little more than a boost to her image. Preoccupied with his business concerns and unwilling to commit himself to one woman, this man spent very little time with Lydia. He would often break dates at the last minute and weeks would go by without a phone call from him.

You might ask, "What's wrong with dating rich, handsome, suave men?" In itself, nothing. Once again, the problem was a loss of perspective. Lydia was devastated when the man didn't call her. She would become insanely jealous and suffered great emotional pain in trying to sustain the relationship. And she never stopped to think about what she was getting on a personal level from this outwardly impressive relationship. Had she done so, she would have realized that she was getting very little.

Combating Love Slobism

Your value, of course, is contingent on far more than whether or not somebody else cares about you or holds you in esteem. Try to distinguish between "who I am" and "what I do." What you do is your tennis game, your political acumen, your scores on the SATs, your ability (based on personality, physical attractiveness, and intelligence) to attract a man who will love you. Those strengths and weaknesses are very different from who you are, what your value is as a human being. Your value as a human being is the sum total of thousands of attributes and liabilities, the strengths and weaknesses that make up your uniqueness as a person. There is no conceivable way that any one person could determine what each of those assets and liabilities is worth. None of these bits of data are measurable in terms of relative worth by any standard whatsoever. To value or devalue yourself based on only one bit of information—someone else's feelings about you—is a distinctly erroneous cognitive belief. Most love slobs magnify and overvalue the notion that their worth is largely dependent on one factor alone: whether or not someone else loves and cares about them. They may be successful at work, be a loyal friend, and play a mean game of tennis, but in their distorted "worth weighing," those things hardly count at all.

To bail out of a bad relationship, you have to stop valuing yourself on the basis of whether or not your relationship is successful. You have to stop denigrating yourself whenever your relationship goes bad. You have to get off that emotional roller coaster in which whenever you feel you are in a good relationship—that is, the person seems to love and value you—you feel up, but whenever you are in a bad relationship—that is, the person seems to devalue you—you feel down. Your emotions cannot rise and fall dependent on whether or not he loves you. You might be a volunteer paramedic, but if he doesn't love you, despite your unselfish work to help save lives, you define yourself as worthless.

This argument may seem obvious, but it's an error of thinking that many, many people fall into.

Combating Contingent Self-Acceptance: Self-Value Checklist

In a column on the left side of a piece of paper, list the qualities you have valued about yourself in the past and value about yourself now, as well as qualities others have suggested are your valuable characteristics. Examples of these qualities would be "I am generous," "I'm a good parent," and "I have a great sense of humor."

In the column on the right, list only one quality: "My partner loves me very much."

Look at these two columns and ask yourself whether the column on the right truly outweighs all of the other things about you that are valuable. Then ask yourself, Is there any legitimate way I can rate or weigh each of these positive characteristics about myself? The answer, of course, will be no. There is no objective rating. Now you can see the absurdity of the cognitive belief that all your personal value is based on whether or not one person loves you.

Combating Overconcern with Your Public Image: Real Life Challenges

You can challenge your overconcern with your public image using a technique cognitive behavior therapists call "vicarious modeling." For example, if you are afraid to go out alone to a movie or to a restaurant when your boyfriend or husband is unavailable or if you have ignored your friends and have been reluctant to make dates with them on the possible chance that your boyfriend might want to see you, you can begin challenging these inhibitions by rehearsing positive alternatives in your mind. Picture yourself going to a movie theater or to dinner alone or telling your boyfriend that you need time with your friends. As your fears and discomforts emerge, feed yourself comforting key phrases such as, "I can make it," "Everything about me is not dependent on this man's love," "Yes, this is uncomfortable, but I can get through it," "People are not sitting in judgment of me. The two couples sitting next to me in the theater couldn't care less that I'm here alone. As a matter of fact, they might actually admire my ability to go out and be independent." See yourself doing each of these activities with confidence and pleasure.

After you have successfully combated your discomfort during the visualizations, you can perform the actual act in real life, gradually increasing the discomfort level of the situation. Go out to a movie theater. The first time, sit in a back row. The next time you go to the theater, sit somewhere in a more conspicuous section. The third time, you might sit next to two couples. When you become uncomfortable, feed yourself comforting self-statements as you did during the vicarious modeling exercise. (More detailed instructions for performing deep relaxation and vicarious modeling are given in chapter 5.)

You might also experiment with telling your most image-conscious friend that you have started dating a rather poor, plain-looking fellow. See how she reacts and *how you react to her*. It may be that your image-conscious friend will not react as terribly as you expect. If she does, you have a good opportunity to assert the positive qualities of this man. Taking this risk will demonstrate to you that the sky will not fall in. You will not lose your friend if you date someone who is not considered a "catch." And if you do, you might question the value of that friendship.

Are You Risk Adverse?

Another reason why many people stay stuck in unhappy relationships is because they are afraid to take chances. They are what we call "risk adverse." Why don't you leave? What are you afraid of? How hard are you going to have to work to free yourself? How risk adverse are you? In your life thus far you have developed either an adventurous spirit or a fear of risking and doing new things. Again, this style is usually learned from one's parents and reinforced by life experience. Some of you operate from the mainstay belief, "No pain, no gain." The assumption here is that you have to take chances if you want something from life.

Some of you grew up with a very different philosophy, one that could be described as an exaggerated adherence to the adage, "Look before you leap." If you look hard enough and long enough, leaping usually doesn't seem like a good idea.

The following test will help you evaluate how willing you are to take risks, such as bailing out of your relationship. Rate your responses by the following method:

1 = strongly diagree
2 = disagree
3 = neither agree nor disagree

4 = agree
5 = strongly agree

_____ I welcome change.
_____ I consider myself an adventurer.
_____ I enjoy fantasizing about separating from my partner.
_____ The thought of being alone without my partner does not frighten me.
_____ I do not make excuses for my partner's negative behavior.
_____ I usually get what I want.
_____ Breaking up a long-time relationship is not necessarily a personal failure.
_____ The way I feel about myself is independent of the success of my relationship.
_____ In the past, when I've recognized a relationship was dead, I was able to end it and move on.
_____ If I lose this relationship, I will surely at some time have another relationship.

Now add up your score. If you get a score of forty to fifty, you are a risk taker. There is no doubt in your mind that you will survive if you bail out. If you get a score of thirty to thirty-nine, you are daring at times, but at other times you fear taking a risk. You are aware of the importance of a relationship to your ultimate happiness but you know you can survive letting go, although with some emotional cost. If you get a score of twenty to twenty-nine, relationships are counting too much. You probably remain in relationships longer than you should. If you get a score of ten to nineteen, you're very risk adverse. *Keep reading this book.*

If you are risk adverse and stuck in an unhappy relationship, you are living in a perpetual state of comfortable discomfort.
Figure 1 (page 111) is a "map" illustrating various zones of comfort and discomfort relative to being able to take risks. Basically, if you are risk adverse, you have been living in the land of "Comfortable Discomfort," the land of the risk adverse, pop-

ulated by whiners and procrastinators. Your goal is to take up citizenship in the land of the risk takers, the country called "Freedom from Fear." To pass from Comfortable Discomfort to Freedom from Fear, you must pass through the border, known as the "Zone of Discomfort." When you pass through this zone, you must overcome the challenge of two major obstacles—the "Mountains of Fearful Anticipation" and the "What If Border Police" who patrol the zone and question you. "What will happen to you there?" they ask. "You won't be able to live in a new state." "You'll be alone, in unfamiliar territory." "You'll feel fear." "You'll feel shame," are some of their other admonitions. Safe passage is ensured by following the advice of this book and *doing the suggested exercises*. Although you will experience initial discomfort, passing through the Zone of Discomfort will change you from a whiner and procrastinator to a healthy risk taker.

In other words, you have two choices: You can maintain your citizenship, perpetually stalled by the mountains and the border police that are your enslaving patterns and beliefs, or you can move to another country, the land of Freedom from Fear, where you learn new beliefs and patterns of behavior. The exercises we have developed for you in chapter 5 will guide you safely through your passage to the land of Freedom from Fear.

Do You Live with the Fantasy That It Will All Change?

Many of you avoid bailing out of a bad relationship because you remain mired in hopes: "He'll finally understand me." "He'll fully approve of me." "He'll love me." "He'll stop his abuse." Or "If I'm good, he'll be good." You follow a kind of magical thinking based on "a hidden bargain." You operate according to the rules of this hidden bargain wherein you

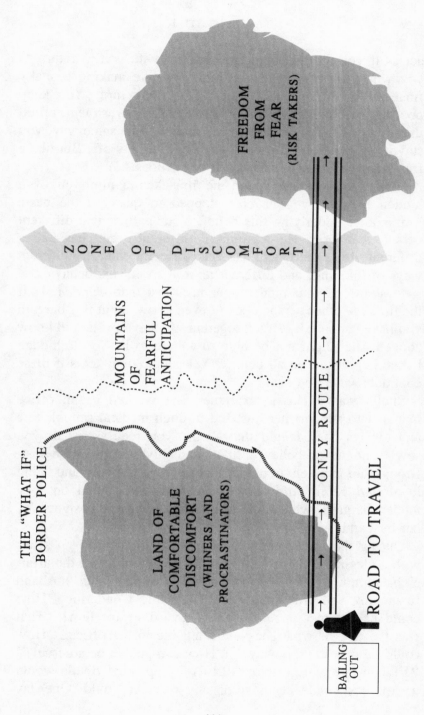

THE "WHAT IF" BORDER POLICE

MOUNTAINS OF FEARFUL ANTICIPATION

ZONE OF DISCOMFORT

FREEDOM FROM FEAR (RISK TAKERS)

LAND OF COMFORTABLE DISCOMFORT (WHINERS AND PROCRASTINATORS)

ONLY ROUTE

ROAD TO TRAVEL

BAILING OUT

act as if your partner signed a contract with you to return to you what you have given to him. It's like making a shaky financial investment and waiting for the return. You keep pouring more and more money into that bad investment, afraid that if you withdraw, you will lose it all. In the same way, you stay in the relationship, waiting for it all to pay off. But like a fraudulent investment scheme, it never does.

When you operate under the mistaken assumption of a hidden bargain, you haven't stopped to question the basic irrationality underlying this belief. Your partner is a different person than you. He was raised differently and has had a different life experience. He has different values, different ways of thinking, and different reinforcers for his behavior.

In addition, your hidden agenda is just that—*hidden*. Half the time the other person doesn't even know about this bargain you have supposedly struck together. And even if he did know about it, he might not be able to adhere to it. So the hidden bargain is absurd on all counts. Yet people operate as if these contracts were iron clad.

Sheila was a classic example. She worked as an office manager to support her husband through medical school. She had always been taught that "what you reap, so shall you sow" and never believed that good guys could finish last. Brought up in an environment that reinforced giving and being loyal *and being paid back in kind,* Sheila signed on to a hidden bargain, which, of course, had not been cosigned by her husband.

During the third year of medical school, he had an affair with a classmate. Even when Sheila found out about the affair eight months later, she continued to support her husband financially and emotionally, all the while wondering "How could he not recognize all that I have done for him?" That was the text of what she would tell me in the office. "How could he hurt me this way?" "How can people be so cruel?" "I'm sure he will grow out of this." Typically, Sheila would try to substantiate her position any way she could. One day she brought me an article from a so-called women's magazine that discussed the number of married men who have affairs during medical school. The article asserted that these men usually lose interest in these affairs. Sheila, of course, planned on her husband losing interest in his affair, but he moved out of the home in his fourth year of school to live with his other woman. Even then Sheila had a hard time believing her relationship was over and that she had been taken.

Many women I've seen who have come to me after their husbands have left them are like Sheila. They can't believe it. It wasn't supposed to work out like this. They had the idea that if they keep on providing their nurturance, money, and loyalty, they would be paid back, with dividends. And, of course, that's predicated on a belief in the fairness of the universe, an unfortunate illusion that they must let go.

As Dr. Albert Ellis, the noted psychologist, has pointed out numerous times, the notion that the universe is fair and metes out good and bad luck equally is usually a *demand* that life be fair, rather than an honest appraisal based on facts and observation. The reality is that the universe and the world are not fair. People who do good do *not* necessarily get good in return. They may wish it, they may prefer it. But to demand it is to set themselves up for terrible disappointment when the world acts the way the world will anyway, distributing good and bad luck with total disregard for a person's goodness or badness.

The naive notion that the universe operates under a code of ethics can be traced back to childhood myths. For example, every Christmas little boys and girls expect presents from Santa Claus as rewards for being good. Or they learn that if they get all their spelling words right, they'll be rewarded with an *A* and a gold star. Later in life, we learn that many people who work hard do not get rewards—the job or the promotion. Many people who are very loving do get cheated on. That doesn't mean that hard work can't improve your chances of getting the job or that loyalty doesn't contribute to your being treated lovingly. But nothing is guaranteed. Many people who live with the fantasy that "it will all change," do think deep down that they are guaranteed a return for their efforts.

Many people believe that they have complete control over their relationship. This notion is absolutely crazy. These people think that if they spend time thinking good thoughts, if they do good things, if they turn the other cheek, if they etc., etc., they'll find the right formula and it will get better. But whether or not your relationship succeeds also has a great deal to do with the other person's motivations, expectations, reinforcement history, values, and how these issues interact with your own. Your belief that you have total control is a myth that will perpetuate your frustration and confusion. It will make you miserable because you will persist in the same erroneous cognitive beliefs and, therefore, keep making the same mistakes.

Why do you continue to have these unrealistic fantasies that it will get better? Here are some possible answers.

• *You have seen your parents modeling the very same fantasies and you have incorporated those fantasies and the resultant behaviors into your own adult life.* Polly was married to a drug addict. When I suggested that she keep a log of the kinds of thoughts she would have when her husband would come home high, she reported a primary thought she had not previously recognized as part of her belief system: "He will see how much I love him, and love will win over the addiction. I know I just have to stay with him and demonstrate to him in every way how much I love him, and he will get better." Of course, he didn't get better, and he continued to take more and more advantage of her goodness.

Polly had modeled her behavior after her father, who had explained away her mother's alcoholism by saying, "She'll get better, she'll get over it, she's going through a hard time." But the hard time lasted ten, even twenty years, throughout an entire lifetime.

Polly and her father are typical of many spouses of addicts

and alcoholics. They hang in there, thinking love will conquer all. Of course, it doesn't. It is worthwhile to note, that an entire collection of literature has been recently accumulated on the utter futility of "enabling" the addict.

• *Another reason you may be hanging on to your fantasies that things will get better is that you may still be looking for that elusive formula that would get your critical or emotionally absent parents to approve of you, to love you unconditionally, or even just to pay attention to you.* Your search failed with your parents, but you erroneously assume that your current formula will work with your partner. Despite overwhelming evidence that he is no good for you, you continue to zealously seek out ways to nurture, to love, and to relate to him to get the relationship to work out.

Laurel had a father who was stoic, distant, and uninvolved. When she came to see me, she was nineteen and worked in his retail store. She did everything and anything to please him. She was desperately seeking his approval and acknowledgment. Laurel worked sixteen-hour days, managed all the clerks, did not ask for higher wages, and even spied on her mother, from whom her father was divorced.

Of course, all her efforts were for nothing because her father just didn't have the emotional ability to reach out to her and acknowledge what she was doing for him. Even as a schoolgirl, when she had come home with a disappointing report card, her father didn't demand higher grades. He simply paid little attention to her progress in school or her accomplishments or failures in life in general.

Like many others, Laurel ceaselessly sought a magic formula that would change her father's behavior. When she became older, she kept up this vain pursuit in her romantic relationships. She chose the same kind of men as her dad, stoic and uninvolved types who were just as difficult to please, and she kept redoubling her efforts to gain their attention and appreciation.

Women like Laurel say to themselves, "Somehow I'll find

a way to make him love and approve of me.'' I call this tenacity ''unreasonable missionary zeal.'' When you are stuck in this mode, you are afraid of turning back, of giving up. You are afraid of failure, which to your irrational way of thinking would be horrible. Your persistence suggests that you are still seeking the approval you didn't receive from your parents.

You must totally give up this self-defeating struggle for approval. The fact is that you never could have satisfied your parents or gained their nonjudgmental approval. They set their own irrational standards for you. Or they were so insensitive or disturbed themselves, they could not possibly have provided the acknowledgment for which you yearned.

Do You Suffer from
Low Frustration Tolerance (LFT)?

Many human beings are afflicted with what psychologists call ''low frustration tolerance'' or LFT. If you have LFT, you don't want any problems in your life. No one wants problems, but your response is to avoid rather than to resolve these problems and to get angry, depressed, or anxious if you can't avoid them. Even though you're being hassled and disappointed every day by your partner, the thought of the greater hassles of challenging the situation, of bailing out, and of adjusting to being single overwhelms you. You'll do anything to avoid problems, including staying in an unhappy relationship.

''Discomfort anxiety'' is related to LFT. Discomfort anxiety is simply fear about feeling uncomfortable. All humans avoid feeling uncomfortable to some degree. Procrastinators have great discomfort anxiety. People who are phobic and people who are very unassertive are frequently discomfort anxious.

If you are discomfort anxious, you don't want to feel bad

and you will do anything to avoid discomfort, particularly in your body. Eighty percent of all airplane phobics are not afraid of dying but of losing control of their bodies. They fantasize that somehow when that door closes, they will flip out. They will run up and down the aisle, lose control of their bowels, and generally manifest physically a full-blown anxiety attack. Like the airplane phobic, some of you are less afraid of leaving your partner than of the possibility that you will lose control of yourself without the restraint exerted over you by the relationship. As uncomfortable, or even as miserable, as you might be with this person, being with him represents a kind of safety, a control on your behavior.

Problems are hardly enjoyable, but is a problem-free life a realistic goal? Here's a quick and easy exercise that will ease your discomfort anxiety and your low frustration tolerance. Spend half an hour reviewing your major conflicts or problems over the past few years, such as money problems, social discomfort, work problems, and so on. Think of the effort you made in avoiding and worrying about them. Now recall how these problems worked out. What can you learn from this?

This exercise will help you reflect on problems you didn't want to tackle. It will help you focus on the issues your low frustration tolerance kept you from dealing with. On review of these situations, you will probably see that even without professional help or this book, you were able to get through most of them reasonably well. What did you learn from this? You should be able to recognize that eventually you did overcome your anxiety and achieve some sort of solution.

Another exercise is to choose an activity that is very uncomfortable for you. In my case, every morning when I go into the office there are seven or eight phone calls on my desk that I must return. Invariably, two or three are very uncomfortable for me, either having to do with talking to difficult patients or involving one or another uncomfortable situations. For years, I would put those uncomfortable calls off, placing them on the bottom of the pile. Since I learned more about challenging my discomfort anxiety, I now place them on the top of the pile and I get to them first.

I have learned that the suffering and pain I experience while worrying about situations such as these uncomfortable phone calls is far greater than actually returning these calls and completing the task.

Now what we'd like you to do is to run a movie in your mind of the uncomfortable activity you have chosen, such as cleaning out your closets. See yourself moving through the uncomfortable situation confidently, easily accomplishing the task. Now, reconsider that same overwhelming activity. Break it up into small, manageable parts, such as getting rid of extra hangers or rearranging shoes or putting away clothes that are out of season. Carry out one small part of this activity each day.

Next, choose a more important task, such as looking for a job. Break it up into small, manageable parts, such as putting a résumé together, xeroxing it, compiling a list of job prospects from various sources, setting up appointments for interviews, preparing for the interviews, etc. Keep on selecting progressively more difficult and more important life tasks for the movie-in-your-mind exercise until you are ready to tackle your greatest fear—the fear of bailing out.

CHAPTER 5

Fear of Bailing Out

*F*ear is the single most common reason why people do not bail out. To get out of a bad relationship, you must be able to identify and challenge the fears and their core cognitive components that keep you stuck. Research shows that most fears have an irrational cognitive component, that is, a distorted, dysfunctional belief or idea or outlook. An irrational cognitive component is the basis of every fear you have; it is what fuels it and keeps it viable.

The following is a discussion of common fears people have about the prospect of bailing out. Many of these fears are nonconscious, that is, you may not be aware that you have them and how much they determine your behavior. Most likely, several of these fears are operating at the same time. Do not look at the following list of fears and just check off one. Place a check by any of the fears that apply to you and keep you from acting.

At the end of the description of each fear syndrome we have provided you with a number of healthy counterthoughts to challenge each fear and be used in your counterattack. Later in this chapter you will learn how to apply these counterthoughts in a systematic program. For now, think about each fear, and whether or not it applies to you. Then review the healthy counterthoughts and see how you either agree with them or resist agreeing with them.

The Robinson Crusoe Syndrome

You fear that you can't function or survive alone, that some dreadful consequence will befall you if you try to function independently. You imagine all the horrendous possibilities that will occur when you are stranded on this desert island of aloneness. You will be easily duped, misled, and taken advantage of. You fear that you won't be able to handle the singles scene. You believe that you'll be ridiculed, isolated, and rejected, and will either fail miserably in any new relationships or that no one will want you. You think that something basic and inherent within you is exposed for all to see when you move from being a couple to being on your own. People will reject you because of that inherent flaw, which they will invariably spot. Imagine yourself alone and try to identify the images, thoughts, and ideas that come up to determine whether or not you are plagued by this fear.

Healthy Counterthoughts

Isn't there some evidence from your past that you *have* been able to be on your own without disasterous consequences?

Can't you view this period of aloneness as an extraordinary opportunity to grow as a unique person?

Weren't you reasonably successful when you were last alone?

Didn't at least some people find you attractive?

Isn't it possible that rather than losing those skills and attributes, you have actually become better skilled at negotiating the singles world *because* of what you have learned from your failed relationship?

Is there really any evidence that a fatal flaw has developed?

Perhaps you are temporarily off-stride or feeling particularly vulnerable, but that is a far cry from being permanently flawed.

With the new confidence and assertiveness skills you will gain from this book, isn't there every reason to believe that you will be able to resist those who might try to take advantage of your vulnerability?

Many more healthy thoughts challenging this fear will be provided in an exercise we call "The Fear Buster Chart."

The Once Bit, Twice Shy Syndrome

You fear that a second failure after bailing out would be even more devastating than the first. A second failure would confirm without a shred of doubt that you cannot make it in a relationship. The depression and misery you are experiencing now would become even greater. If you have this fear, you are personalizing the breakup of your relationship far more than you should.

Healthy Counterthoughts

Don't people often fail at projects two, three, or more times until they finally achieve success?

Your tendency right now is to view any future relationship in a negative light because you are in so much turmoil about the failure of your current relationship. You are in so much pain right now that the thought of possibly enduring another breakup in the future is too much to contemplate. But as the pain from this breakup subsides, you will see that there is every reason to believe that your next relationship has a greater probability of succeeding simply because of the insights and skills you will have gained from bailing out.

The Homeless Syndrome

You have some practical fears that revolve around issues such
as the loss of your partner's income and a subsequent drop in
your standard of living. You are convinced that you cannot
make it financially by yourself and that a drop in your standard of living would be intolerable. You are *demanding* that
this standard of living not drop, that it *should* not drop, and
you assume that it would be *terrible* and *catastrophic* if it were
compromised. You have convinced yourself that you couldn't
stand not eating out as often or sitting in the mezzanine rather
than the orchestra. You fear independence and the responsibility of taking care of yourself.

Healthy Counterthoughts

If you had never known about this higher standard of living,
then you certainly would not feel a loss now. Therefore,
it is not a catastrophe but merely a difference to which
you will have to adjust.

You now have a style of living to aspire to.

If one financially secure person found you very desirable,
then it is reasonably probable that there are others who
will too.

In reviewing your talents and past victories, recall that in
the past, before you met your partner, you may have
taken perfectly good care of yourself.

Is there any real, hard evidence that you won't be able to do
this again?

The Old Maid Aunt Syndrome

You fear losing the friends you've made along the way as a
couple. You fear losing the status you've gained by being part
of a couple. You tell yourself erroneously that your only real
worth is being part of a couple. It is really your partner who
attracts people, not you. If you bail out, you will be the loser.

Healthy Counterthoughts

You might have different friends and engage in different activities if you are single, but your basic inherent worth does not depend on whether or not you are part of a couple.

> You might question the value of any friendships that are based not on your inherent worth as an individual but on who you are seen with.
>
> In any case, your status might improve as others see you as someone who is willing to take a risk, get out of an unsatisfying relationship and get on with your life as a single person.

The Black Sheep Syndrome

You fear disapproval from parents, friends, children, relatives, and your partner's parents. You wildly exaggerate what will happen, how these people will treat you, and the impact their reactions will have on your life. You've told yourself, ''They'll disown me'' or ''They'll never talk to me again'' or ''They won't want to be my friend anymore.'' And then you convince yourself that if those things happened, that would be the end of your life. You may also feel extreme guilt that you let them down, as if you should have devoted your whole life to never disappointing others.

Healthy Counterthoughts

> Many people do not talk to their families for many years and survive quite nicely.
>
> In the vast majority of bailing out situations, after an initial period of shock and adjustment, friends and families tend to be supportive and understanding.

You are placing too much importance on yourself if you believe that the rise and fall of your relationship plays such a central role in others' lives. And if others' lives are so devoid of meaning that they ''live'' for your victories and defeats, then they probably have far more problems than you do.

Anyway, so what if some people disapprove of what you've done. Where is it written that *everyone* in the world or even just some significant people *must* approve of your every move?

Will it really make any difference twenty years from now if your friend okayed your breakup? Put it in perspective.

The Never Mind Syndrome

You fear that you will bail out and then suffer lifelong regret for your mistake. You will have an unrelieved obsession, a bleeding wound that will always be open.

Healthy Counterthoughts

You are probably feeling this fear only because you are so locked into the current negative dynamics of this relationship that you can't imagine a future without it. Most likely, however, once you are bailed out, so many new possibilities will open up for you that you won't be likely to look back.

Remember: Even people who were once extremely in love and decimated by a breakup do not suffer regrets for the rest of their lives. The phenomenon of lifelong regret seems to occur more in popular fiction and in the movies than it does in real life.

The Where's My Whipping Boy? Syndrome

You fear that you will no longer be able to blame your lack of success on the relationship. Now, when other aspects of your life don't go well, you blame your lousy relationship. You may begin to realize that perhaps that's just been a diversion, and this knowledge is keeping you from bailing out. You fear that you need the relationship even though you no longer care for him. You may actually feed off the negativity in the relationship, mulling over grievances, scheming and fantasizing revenge, and replaying scenes. Without this relationship, you would feel less alive. It energizes you. You are basically a passionate person whose life has been like a grade-B Italian movie. Something about the fighting and backbiting is terribly important to you. Or you may fear that without the "interesting problem" of your unhappy relationship to discuss, you will no longer get attention from your friends. You believe that you have very little else to share with your friends other than the interesting problem of your relationship. Without it, you're afraid that they would find you boring.

Healthy Counterthoughts

This fear usually occurs on a nonconscious level. You are simply not aware of the grip it has on you. You must honestly appraise what is inhibiting your success in other areas of your functioning.

> Why are you not being promoted at work? Are you not playing office politics well?
>
> Why are you losing friends? Are you acting arrogantly or hypercritically? Why is your life not exciting? Have you placed too much of the responsibilty of feeling alive on your relationship?
>
> Why do you think you are boring except when you talk about your problems? Before you were in your unhappy relationship, did your friends refuse to talk to you?

You must fight the tendency to blame all your problems on the relationship. If you continue to blame your problems on the relationship, you will have learned nothing about moving ahead in life.

The Last Chance Syndrome

You fear you will never find someone else. You think that you are basically an undesirable creep and that you lucked into this relationship. With such low self-esteem, you attribute your current relationship to pure good fortune. Because no one will ever want you again, your logic goes, you have to hold on to this man.

Or you fear that no one else will ever be as attracted to you as the partner you have now or make love to you as well. You may still be physically drawn to your partner even though the relationship is unfulfilling, even destructive. You may have powerful feelings toward him. Not only that, you are used to him.

Healthy Counterthoughts

The belief that this relationship is your last chance is obviously an unfounded fear. You found this man and most likely have had other relationships in your past. There is no reason to believe that you won't be able to form new attachments. There are probably hundreds of thousands of men within your own state who would be equally or more compatible with you. All you have to do is find them.

There is no evidence that your sex life must end after bailing out. Ask yourself, "Why does my next partner *have* to be a fabulous lover?" Isn't it possible that you placed a very high value on sex because there was little else in your relationship to sustain you? Perhaps by focusing on allowing *yourself* more pleasure in bed and not depending solely on your partner you'll take the pressure off any new relationships.

We're all members of the human species. There are no gods roaming this earth capable of bringing you superhuman pleasure. Stop empowering your partner with unique lovemaking abilities. If you had a good sex life with him, chances are you will again with someone else.

Nobody's Grass Is Green Syndrome

You assume that everybody's relationship stinks. Speaking with friends has led you to conclude that no one is really happy in their relationship. Everyone is just tolerating their pain or indifference. You have learned to accept this and make the best of it. The fear is that because no relationship ever works anyway, why go from something that is known into something that is unknown?

Healthy Counterthoughts

The fact that friends occasionally complain about their relationships is certainly no proof that there aren't many qualitatively happier relationships than yours.

Friends also don't always tell the complete truth, especially if they believe that you are suffering and they don't want to make you feel worse.

And anyway, so what if it *is* true that no relationship works out? Isn't it possible that even a series of enjoyable relationships that eventually end in disappointment might be better than hanging on to your current misery for the next twenty years?

The Sand Castle Syndrome

You've spent a lifetime together building wealth, hopes, family, and friends. You just can't see tearing it all down. You fear throwing out everything that was ever important in your life.

Healthy Counterthoughts

All that you have built is not lost. Your children are still yours, as are many of your material possessions, friends, and so on. Your life is not being torn down, merely shifted around and restructured. You haven't been enjoying your joint accomplishments very much anyway. Why won't you just accept that some people simply grow incompatible and move on? Stop irrationally *demanding* that this *one* love go on forever. That's for the storybooks and not for real life.

The Comfort Junkie Syndrome

You fear it's going to get ugly, down, and dirty, and you tell yourself, "I can't go through the horror." You habitually avoid difficult situations and you hate hassles. You probably scored poorly on some of the tests in previous chapters of this book concerning discomfort anxiety. You always avoid discomfort. You believe in the *mañana* ("tomorrow" in Spanish) principle, and tend to put things off.

Healthy Counterthoughts

First, reread the section on risk taking in this book. Ask yourself, "How bad could it *really* get?"

Can things really get that much worse than they already are, or would the storm of bailing out precede the calm of finally being out of your unhappy relationship?

You'll have advisers such as friends, attorneys, and, if needed, professional counselors, to help cushion any blows.

Also, you need to understand that much of the anger and hurt your partner may express is transitory and reflects his momentary anger and outrage. This will most likely pass quickly.

If you put off bailing out, the rage and hurt will just accrue and be even worse further on down the road.

The Weak Sister Syndrome

You may be afraid that your partner will convince you to stay and all your efforts to bail out will come to nothing. You've been so compliant for so long that you've convinced yourself you are too weak to stand up to your partner. You've been down so long you don't know how to get up.

Or perhaps you are afraid to tell the truth, to say what you honestly feel and think. You may have been indirect and dishonest in your life. You may have been afraid of disapproval, of being put down, of being taken advantage of, of being confronted, particularly when you state how you honestly feel and think. Your fear is that if you are truly honest, you will be rejected or you may incur violent anger.

Healthy Counterthoughts

You have to find some opportunities, even in situations that do not involve your partner, to practice assertiveness and to demonstrate to yourself that you can stand up to people.

Remember: Righteous indignation and the belief in your principles can bolster your assertiveness against a stronger, more dominant personality.

If you have gone further this time than ever before in your efforts to bail out, you can begin to give up being compliant and become more courageous. Your partner's disapproval and his put-downs should be viewed as an opportunity to learn. Every negative comment is not a disaster. Negative comments are also perfect opportunities to practice assertiveness skills. For example, don't lock horns with him if he puts you down. Merely restate what you think he has said and then tell him that you have to do what you feel is right for you.

There are two more fears to list here. They are so important that we have saved them for the Fear Buster Chart. Read them over and then think of your own healthy counterthoughts. Write them down. As you read the Fear Buster Chart, compare your list of healthy counterthoughts to those we give you.

The Ogre Syndrome

You're afraid of hurting the other person. You've been unassertive all of your life. You've always turned the other cheek to protect others' feelings even if it means your feelings will be trampled on. You've learned to mistake politeness for unassertiveness, a basic error many people fall into. You exaggerate the amount of pain and the harmful effects your leaving will have on your partner. In fact, his possible pain weighs heavier on you than your own discomfort.

Think of your own healthy conterthoughts.

The Pied Piper Syndrome

You fear the impact that bailing out will have on your children. You are afraid that by bailing out, you will be leading your children down the path to destruction. You wildly exaggerate the effect bailing out will have on your kids, and you obsessively devour every publication that supports your contention. You find yourself drawn to people and articles that confirm your notion that you are damaging your children for life.

Now, try to come up with your own healthy counterthoughts, to these two fears.

On paper, write down any other fears you may have.

Look at the fears you checked off as well as the fears you may have added to the list. What is the likelihood of each of these fears coming true? Go over each fear. How *horrible* would it be if it did occur? What would *actually* happen to you? How would it *actually* affect your life? Let's find out!

The "I Can't Stand It" Mentality

People operate under the belief that if one of their fears came true, they "wouldn't be able to stand it." "I can't tolerate it," they insist. In cognitive behavior therapy we challenge that belief. Of course you can tolerate it. Yes, it would probably be uncomfortable. Certainly it wouldn't be pleasant, but there's very little evidence that you wouldn't be able to tolerate it. There are human beings tolerating it all over the world, all the time. They are tolerating being alone, being guilty, being afraid, being sad.

The key here is to develop incontrovertible evidence that not only can you tolerate it, but you could possibly even blossom as you challenge each of your fears.

The Fear Buster Chart

The Fear Buster Chart is a way to provide yourself with ammunition in the form of healthy thoughts and effective behaviors to defeat the fears that block you from acting. The chart will help you realize that nothing in reality could be worse than the scenarios dreamed up by your own fearful imagination. **This chart is one of the most important exercises in this book.** We will refer to it again and again. *Do not simply read the following section. Interact with it as you would with a therapist.*

Because you are bound to have more than one fear around an issue such as bailing out, look at your list again and choose your five most severe fears.

If you have difficulty identifying your strongest fears, run a movie in your head of your bailing out. Carefully review what you tell yourself about bailing out during the visualization. This will help you identify your five primary fears. Take your time and try to identify the actual nature of each fear.

If you are still stuck, ask close friends to tell you what kinds of fearful statements you have made in the past about bailing out. The following exercise will also help you pinpoint your fears concerning bailing out.

Complete the following sentence and do it several times in succession, quickly, without thinking about your answers first: "When I think about bailing out, I get scared about ————." Free associate the completion of this sentence about bailing out into a tape recorder. Now match up your free association with the list of fears in this chapter and identitfy those fears that seem most threatening.

Take a large piece of paper or oaktag and divide it from left to right into five columns. This will become your Fear Buster Chart.

Column One: List a fear you checked off from the list of fears. For example, we will demonstrate how the chart works with the first fear, The Robinson Crusoe Syndrome. People with this syndrome fear that they can't function or survive alone. We will use this fear to demonstrate many different techniques for coping with and alleviating the fears that keep you from acting.

Column Two: List the cognitions or thoughts about that fear. These are the distorted and incorrect thoughts that lead to inaction. They occur automatically, quickly, and often without complete awareness. Unless you grab these thoughts in the moment, they tend to pass by your consciousness. The key that you are having the thought is that you are also experiencing a mild to profound feeling of discomfort. (It may take the form of anxiety, sadness, or anger.) Some of the distorted thoughts related to the fear listed in column one (in this example, the fear that you can't function or survive alone) might be the following:

"I'll be constantly lonely."
"I'll be alone for the rest of my life."
"I'll be persona non grata within my previous social groups."
"I'll be depressed and unhappy, and little else will ever give me pleasure again."

What are your thoughts that fuel this fear? Write them down in column two.

Column Three: How unrealistic are these distorted thoughts? Here we replace the distorted thoughts with healthier corrected perspectives—replacement beliefs. Here you attack the catastrophizing, the self-condemnation, and the absolutist thinking and find saner, less self-defeating ways of thinking about the matter.

Ask yourself, "Is there evidence to support the truth of the beliefs in column two? Or does the proof show that these are illogical conclusions?"

Corrected perspectives that would replace the distorted thoughts of column two might include the following:

"Alone" and "lonely" are different. Many people spend much time alone but don't feel particularly lonely.

There are many friends and acquaintances who value me as an individual, not only because of my relationship.

I can make new friends. Although that process may be difficult and awkward, it is surely *not* impossible.

I can survive the disapproval of others. Not *everyone* must love me.

These kinds of depressions are usually short lived. I have had the resources to give myself pleasure in the past. It is unlikely that ability will end with the relationship.

Can you think of more healthy thoughts? List them in column three.

Column Four: Do you really believe in the new healthy thoughts, or do you believe *emotionally* more in your fear and the thoughts about the fear? This is a common complaint of patients in cognitive behavior therapy. They understand the corrected perspective *intellectually,* but they can't translate it into a *gut-level conviction.* Many people are of two minds about various thoughts and perspectives. For example, if you grew up believing that you'll have bad luck every time you walk under a ladder, even after you have challenged the emotional, superstitious aspect of that belief as an adult, you may still find yourself feeling uncomfortable when you walk under a ladder. You can be of two minds for a long time about any one fear. It takes constant practice of alternative healthy thoughts, of finding evidence that the distorted beliefs are incorrect, and real-life experiences to change long-held erroneous ideas and beliefs. Even after a great deal of practice and experience, you may still have vestiges of emotional discomfort around certain beliefs and thoughts. But that should not stop you from facing the fear and acting directly. It should not keep you from challenging the irrationality of your beliefs and life rules. If you continually do this, you will become progressively more free and liberated.

In column four you rate your level of belief in the new healthy thoughts on a scale from one to three as follows:

1 = disbelief ("I've written it down but I don't believe it at all.")

2 = intellectual belief and emotional disbelief ("I'm of two minds. I believe it intellectually, but I can't translate that belief into my feelings.")

3 = belief ("I have adopted this belief and made it my own. I have found plenty of evidence to support it.")

Column Five: What has to happen to strengthen your belief in the corrected perspective? List the experiences that will help you better believe in the new perspective *on a gut level*.

Here are some experiences that will help you better believe in the healthy replacement thoughts of column three:

• *"Alone" and "lonely" are different. Many people spend much time alone but don't feel particularly lonely.* To increase your belief in this corrected perspective, you can spend several hours by yourself at formal group or spectator activities. Go to a party or to the movies alone. This extends the period of time you spend by yourself to attending group activities alone. It gives you the opportunity and time to control the feelings of panic, fearfulness, depression, and loneliness you might experience.

You can learn to control these feelings by practicing various coping and relaxation exercises in which you talk to yourself and calm yourself down. The key for these activities is what we call "slow successive approximations," go slowly, step by step. First, you will learn to *visualize* increasingly severe anxiety-provoking experiences (in this case longer and longer periods of time at a party alone). As you hold these images in your mind, you feed yourself coping self-statements. You are extending the time in which you are alone, and you are recognizing that you don't have to feel lonely. It's manageable, it's doable, and you can control the emotions you anticipated would overwhelm you. When you are able to reassure yourself with these statements, then you actually practice these exercises in real life, using the same coping self-statements whenever you need them to reassure yourself. This technique is explained in detail later in this chapter under the heading "Systematic Desensitization."

• *There are many friends and acquaintances who value me as an individual, not only because of my relationship.* To increase your belief in this corrected perspective you can openly question your friends and acquaintances about whether you are valued as an individual or because of your partnership.

You might approach a couple with whom you and your partner have been friendly and make the following statement: "I need to get some feedback from you on something that is very important to me. I need you to be very honest with me even if you're concerned that something you say might hurt me. I know that being with John and me has been rewarding to both of you. If we were no longer together, what would be the future of my relationship with you two? What I'm asking is how would you feel about continuing your relationship with me?"

It's very possible that you won't trust their answer. They may say, "We love you a lot, you're terrific. Of course, we would still want to see you." But if your self-esteem is low at this point or if you think they might be uncomfortable in admitting that your breakup would create an awkward situation for them, you might look for more than verbal reassurance. If appropriate, you might then ask them to plan a date with you without your partner.

You can begin to collect evidence concerning your worth outside of your relationship to your friends. First of all, take a look at when these people became your friends. Didn't many of these friendships begin before your relationship started? Review some of the conversations you've had with these people privately about how much they value *you* as an individual independent of your relationship. The problem with so

many people who are afraid of bailing out is that they act as if
they have incontrovertible evidence that they will be abandoned by their friends. In fact, after questioning and collecting
information, they discover that is not the case.

You can go out socially by yourself and *objectively* discover
if you fit in with the same social group you are convinced is
going to reject you. Take a look. Are you really being rejected, or are you needlessly carrying this fear into the social
situation?

• *I can make new friends. Although that process may be
difficult and awkward, it is surely not impossible.* You can
make new friends and survive the disapproval of others. There
are strategies you can learn for various situations. For example, if you are at a party, you can join a group of people who
are conversing by first listening in and identifying the common
themes with which you are familiar and then jumping in.

Relaxation and Other Antifear Techniques

The following techniques (e.g., relaxation, systematic desensitization, blowup, pleasuring experiences, and shame attack
exercise) are all designed to help facilitate your belief in the
correct perspectives developed in your Fear Buster Chart.

You can accept and incorporate alternative beliefs much
more clearly when you are relaxed. You are more open for
"reprogramming," for taking in suggestions on new patterns
of thought and behavior that will eventually replace the old,
worn out, depressing, negative patterns. Fear and depression
are often so horrendous and distracting that it is impossible to
attend to and integrate new healthier thoughts and to attempt
new corrective behaviors.

Research has shown that for deep relaxation or meditation
to be effective, you must have at least one period of relaxation
daily, lasting a minimum of fifteen to twenty minutes. Train-

ing begins by focusing on breathing and muscle relaxation and then moves on to letting thoughts come in rather than harboring any worrisome thoughts you already have. It does not matter what form of relaxation you employ. What matters is that you have a consistent and deep experience of relaxation. In such a state, thoughts occur less frequently and do not become fixations. Your breathing becomes slow and regular, and muscles are experienced as deeply relaxed. This state might be characterized by a heavy, weighty sense of your body, or the opposite—you may feel a light, floating sensation. People often report feeling quiet, focused, and passive. All these sensations are usually indications of being deeply relaxed.

The following is only one of the many techniques that can bring you to this desired state of deep relaxation. It is important that you understand a relaxation period means time alone in a quiet environment where you will not be disturbed, even by the telephone or doorbell. It does not mean lying back on the sofa with your feet up, gazing at the tube and holding a can of beer. During deep relaxation, you are to refrain from any other activity.

Contraction-Release or Progressive Relaxation

One of the most common methods of relaxation is based on the principle of *contraction-release* in which you tense successive muscle groups of your body and then let go. As you tense a group of muscles, hold them as tightly as possible, then let go and relax completely. Best results are gained through regular practice. If you wish, you can tape record these instructions, or have a friend record them. Listening to calming music while doing any of the relaxation exercises can be helpful.

Begin by arranging your body in a comfortable, receptive position. Lying on your back on the floor is preferable, but you may sit in a chair if you wish. Uncross your legs and extend your arms, palms facing up.

Take three long, full breaths, exhaling completely with each breath. Feel your body letting go of tension with each exhalation.

Clench your right fist and hold the tension there, tighter and tighter. Study the tension in your right fist as you keep the rest of your body relaxed. Then drop the tension in your right fist and allow the sensation of relaxation to flow in. Observe the difference between relaxation and tension as a pleasant, heavy feeling of relaxation flooding your hand—into your palm, into each finger.

Now clench your left fist and then release the tension in the same manner as above.

Clench both fists and straighten both arms, tensing the muscles in both arms. Hold the tension. Observe the tension. Now release the tension in both arms and let them drop to your sides. Observe the warm, heavy feeling of relaxation flowing into your arms, down the elbows, through the wrists, into the palms. Feel yourself letting go, relaxing. Take a long, deep breath. Exhale slowly, becoming even more relaxed.

Take another long, deep breath, filling your lungs. Hold the air in your chest, observing the tension created. Now exhale slowly, observing the walls of your chest loosen as the air is pushed out. Continue relaxing and breathing freely and gently.

Tighten your abdominal muscles by pushing them up and out as far as they can go. Hold the tension there and study it. Release the abdominal muscles and allow the feeling of relaxation to flow into each muscle. Continue breathing freely and easily. Each time you exhale, notice the pleasant sensation of relaxation spreading throughout your body.

Tense your buttocks and thighs by pressing down as hard as you can and by pinching your buttocks muscles together. Hold the tension and study it. Release and allow a deep, soothing feeling of relaxation to flow in.

Tense your lower legs by pressing both feet down and pushing your toes away from your face. Hold the tension in your legs and feet. Release the tension and allow rejuvenating relaxation to flow in. Breathe in and out easily and allow relaxation to flow throughout your body.

Tense your back and shoulders by pinching your shoulders together and arching your back off the floor. Hold the tension and then let go, allowing your back to drop to the floor and feeling relaxation spread.

Roll your head back and forth very gently from side to side, releasing the muscles in the back of your neck.

Tense your facial muscles by sticking out your tongue as far as it will go, closing your eyes tightly, and wrinkling up your forehead. Hold the tension, then release, allowing warm relaxation to flow through the scalp, forehead, eyelids, cheeks, jaw, even the tongue.

Now allow your body to experience heaviness, as if it were boneless and only the floor is keeping you from sinking. You may, at this time, make a mental inventory of the parts of your body you have contracted and released, telling yourself as you go through your body that each part is heavy, warm, and relaxed, thereby allowing your relaxation to go even deeper.

When you are ready to enter the waking state, begin by gently wriggling toes and fingers, gradually moving into whatever larger stretches your body seems to want. Roll to one side in a fetal position, place one palm on the ground, and push off to lift your body into a sitting position.

Autogenic Training

Another successful method of achieving a deep state of relaxation is called "autogenic training." The following is a suggested procedure for this method.

1. Assume a comfortable position. Lying on your back is best because it tends to minimize distractions. If you feel discomfort in your lower back, it is often helpful to place pillows behind the knees to elevate them slightly. You may want to use a pillow under your head, as well.

2. Begin a steady flow of suggestions to your dominant arm (the right arm if you are right-handed). Start with "my right arm is heavy. . . . My right arm is heavy. . . . I am at peace, and my arm is heavy." Do not pay attention to any distracting thoughts. Allow them to flow out of your mind and continue with a steady, gentle stream of suggestions.

3. After sixty to ninety seconds, mentally contact the left arm. Continue with a steady but casual flow of suggestions: "My left arm is heavy. . . . My left arm is heavy. . . . I am at peace, and my arm is heavy."

4. Continue with the rest of your body, adding a new area every sixty to ninety seconds. Include the right leg, the left leg and the whole body. The entire process will take about eight to ten minutes.

5. Once your entire body has become heavy, discontinue the flow of suggestions and take a few moments to notice any changes that have taken place. The degree of relaxation produced will improve with practice. At first, even a small amount of success is significant.

6. You may repeat the first five steps with the additional suggestion of *warmth* and *heat* in your arms and legs.

7. When you are ready to enter the waking state, begin by gently wriggling toes and fingers, gradually moving into whatever larger stretches your body seems to want. Roll to one side in a fetal position, place one palm on the ground, and push off to lift your body into a sitting position.

Diaphragmatic Breathing

A simple form of relaxation involves only the use of the breath.

Relax your whole body as completely as you can. Breathe in through your nose in a natural, gentle way.

Allow the breath to travel all the way to the bottom of your belly, to the diaphragm muscles. Gently *expand* your belly to take in each breath. Keep your shoulders and chest as still as possible. (It might help you to put one hand on your chest and one hand on your stomach to monitor the movement in your chest and stomach. The goal, of course, is to keep the stomach moving up and down and the chest as quiet as possible.)

Breathe out *slowly* through your mouth, emptying the belly and relaxing the jaw, letting it drop. Breathe out as slowly as you can, making each exhale last. Do not hold your breath between inhalations and exhalations.

Be sure to breathe in a slow, gentle, and natural manner. Do not hyperventilate (rapid breathing that leads to dizziness or light-headedness).

Instructions for Use of Relaxation Techniques

The following instructions have been adapted from material developed by Dr. Steven T. Fishman of the Institute for Behavior Therapy in New York City.

• *Formal Training Period (weeks one to three).* Practice your chosen method of deep relaxation at least once a day. Practice at a time when you are not overly tired and when distractions can be minimized. Dim the lights and lie on a sofa, bed, or floor. The goal is not to fall asleep but to get in touch with feelings and sensations that accompany relaxation. Do not actively attempt to make use of the relaxation in any way during this period.

• *Phasing Period (week four).* During this period, practice as above every other night of the week. On the "off" night, lie on the same sofa, bed, or floor that you have been using for your training under the same environmental conditions, but for a period of time not to exceed ten minutes. During this time attempt to relax yourself by the use of cue words such as *calm, heavy, relaxed,* or by the use of some previously decided emotive imagery. You might imagine a particularly pleasant scene from nature or any image that connotes relaxation to you.

• *Incorporation Period (week five).* During this period use the relaxation procedure you have been following only two times. On all other nights practice merely using the cue words and/or emotive imagery for a period not to exceed ten minutes. More important, however, is that during this period you will begin to use these same cue words or images as you go through your everyday routines, so that relaxation can begin to be incorporated into your normal functioning. You can take fifteen to thirty seconds out of each hour, if possible, to close your eyes and subvocally utter the cue words regardless of your level of activity at the time.

• *Discretionary Period (week six and thereafter).* Use the relaxation procedure at your discretion. Do not use it too often; for the relaxation training to be successful, the skill of relaxing must become yours rather than dependent on whichever of the above formal relaxation procedures you chose to follow. You are urged to continue using the cue words as you go through your everyday routines and to be consciously aware of relaxing any and all muscle groups that are not being actively used for a specific task. Practice relaxing in a variety of situations and circumstances, such as in the shower, sitting on a bus, standing in line, and so on.

Learning how to put yourself in a state of deep relaxation will enable you to practice the following techniques to reduce your fears.

Systematic Desensitization

Systematic desensitization, the most popular fear-reduction technique, has three components: First, getting as relaxed as possible and learning how to call up relaxation on demand. Second, setting up a hierarchy of items in which you rank order your level of fear in various scenes, from least fear producing to most fear producing. Be particularly careful to identify those aspects of the situation that are likely to cause you anxiety and those aspects that are likely to be irrelevant. Be aware that what is frightening for one person may not be for another, and vice versa, so do not attempt to find some arbitrary means of measuring how fear producing an item is *supposed* to be. Your own level of fear is all that matters. For example, some airplane phobics are more likely to be terrified the night before the flight than they are at takeoff. Others are much more terrified at takeoff than they are the night before. You must draw up your own individual hierarchy that is sensitive to *your* particular fears.

Third, while you are in a state of deep relaxation, expose yourself visually to these various anxiety-provoking images in order of ascending anxiety based on what we call "subjective units of disturbance scale" (SUDS). The laws of learning indicate that as you expose yourself to a high-anxiety situation while in a relaxed state and, at the same time, provide yourself with coping self-statements, you greatly reduce the impact of the anxiety by substituting the more adaptive habit (relaxation).

For example, a simple phobia might be being afraid of dogs. Depending on the various idiosyncratic anxiety cues, that is, what exactly about dogs produces fear, the patient will imagine various scenes involving dogs and rank them in order of least to most anxiety producing. If three separate anxiety cues operate within this phobia—the size of the dog, whether the dog is free or on a leash, and how far away the dog is—the first item in the hierarchy might be "I see a small poodle on a leash two blocks away." The second item might be "I see that poodle one block away, and the owner is leaning over to unhook the leash." The third item might be "I see a German shepherd two blocks away." The fourth item might be "I see the poodle running loose and coming quite close to me." The fifth item might be "I see the poodle jumping on my legs." The sixth item might be "I see the poodle licking my hand.'' The seventh item might be ''The German shepherd is running loose near me.'' And the scenes would escalate in intensity accordingly. The person imagines each of these while in a state of relaxation and feeds himself coping self-statements whenever he experiences fear.

Systematic desensitization is also useful for overcoming fears other than phobias, such as the Robinson Crusoe Syndrome, or the fear of being alone, as well as other fears of bailing out. The following are the steps you could take in carrying out a systematic desensitization of your fear of being alone.

Draw up a list of all the various anxiety-producing stimuli associated with being alone. Some of these items will be low-level anxiety and others, high level. Here are some examples:

''I am alone on a Saturday night and no one is calling me.''
''I reach out to a friend and she tells me that she's busy that night.''
''I'm sick with a stomach flu and there's no one there to help me.''
''I'm reading an ad about a wonderful trip to the Caribbean. As I'm reading, I begin to get anxious because I see it's designed for couples, not singles.''
''I'm at a wedding. I've been accustomed to bringing my partner, and now I have to go alone. Everyone else is part of a couple. I feel overwhelmed by anxiety and it's getting out of control.''
''I'm walking through a park and everybody around seems to be in couples. I begin to experience anxiety and tension.''
''I'm in a movie theater alone surrounded by couples. They seem to be looking in my direction and commenting.''

Now list the above scenes and any others you imagine in hierarchal order, beginning with least to most anxiety producing. Remember, those scenes *you* find most anxiety producing might not affect others as profoundly. Different people have different trigger situations. How do you know a situation produces anxiety in you? First of all, you know which situations are likely to bother you the most by real-life experiences. If you have avoided certain situations or feel a flood of anxiety when you contemplate those situations, they are clearly anxiety producing for you. You may look over your list and ask yourself, "Which of these situations have occurred in my life and bothered me the most?" Another way to determine if a situation is anxiety producing is to close your eyes and imagine the situation. Tune in closely to how you feel. Is there a quickening in your breathing? Is there an increase in your heartbeat? Are there knots in your stomach? Are your shoulders tense? Do you feel a tinge of a headache?

After you have set up the hierarchy of scenes, assign each of the items a SUDS rating from 1 to 10, depending on how tense each scene makes you feel.

Go through the first scene while in a state of deep relaxation. Imagine the item as clearly as you can. See it as if it were happening at that very moment. Hold the scene for at least one minute. Use any anxiety you experience as a signal or prompt to drop the scene and go back into deep relaxation by cue words or images (such as *release* or *calm*). Relax your muscles, deepen your breathing, calm your mind. Reintroduce the scene. Now use your anxiety as a means to identify your self-defeating thoughts. What are you telling yourself that is frightening you? Once you have done that, find a healthy replacement thought. These new cognitions can come from your Fear Buster Chart under the third column. Relax again and then reimagine the scene. Repeat the process as long as necessary. Once you are able to expose yourself to the scene three consecutive times for about one minute each without experiencing significant anxiety, you have met the desensitization criteria and can move on to the next scene.

Visualization may be a problem for you. There are two ways to visualize. Let's say you are imagining yourself in a roller coaster riding up and down the curves. You can either see yourself standing on the ground, observing yourself in the roller coaster, or you can imagine yourself sitting in the front seat of the roller coaster itself, feeling the wind blowing across your face, feeling the sense of movement, and screaming.

Obviously, the second type of visualization is preferable because it is more immediate and, therefore, more real. You are not observing yourself, but actually going through the process and experiencing your anxiety.

The Blowup Technique

Another helpful technique for busting fears is called the "blowup technique." In the blowup technique you imagine the situation you fear and make the scenario even worse than you expect. For example, if you are afraid of your friends' rejection, you can imagine your friends walking around you with boldly lettered picket signs reading, We Don't Want Anything to Do with Sheila because She's Not with Bob Anymore! You can actually generate humorous, absurd, exaggerated images. If you can create an absurd image around the fear, it tends to make the reality far less frightening. According to learning theory, when this technique is repeated over a period of time, the fear is gradually extinguished.

Pleasuring Experiences

To increase your belief in the corrected idea that your ability to give yourself pleasure does not end with the relationship, you can learn to set up "pleasuring experiences." List ten or twelve pleasurable experiences you had on your own or with friends while you were in the relationship or before you entered into it. You may have abondoned these pleasures now that you are feeling sad and anxious. Assign yourself to try one of these pleasuring experiences each week. Patients have done such things as gone horseback riding, visited an amusement park, bought a collectible at an auction, camped out on a beach, had a day at the movies, window shopped, or gone to a free concert in the park. Engaging in this kind of activity will begin the process of building positive reinforcement and returning pleasure into your life.

Shame Attack Exercises

To increase your belief in the healthy idea that you can survive the disapproval of others, you can practice various "assertiveness exercises," simple acts such as asking someone to stop smoking, or what we call "shame attack exercises." Dr. Albert Ellis first used this term more than twenty years ago. A typical example of a shame attack exercise would be to go out in the street and ask someone for change for a quarter. After the person gives you change, you say, "Thank you, but I changed my mind and I'd like the quarter back." Another example would be to go into a large department store and announce the time out loud. What usually happens is people look at you, but then you walk out of the store feeling liberated, saying to yourself, "I'm ashamed of being alone, yet here I walk into a store, do something attention getting and totally unconventional, and other than just a moment or two of discomfort, nothing happens to me!" The idea of giving you such an exaggerated assignment is to help you challenge the idea of feeling ashamed of *anything* you do. The key is to challenge the shame that could keep you from bailing out. Shame attack helps put your shame in perspective and short circuits the depression that follows bouts of shame.

That is how the Fear Buster Chart works. Now, let's run another fear through the chart.

Many of you feel that if you bail out, you will damage your children irreparably. The idea that your children will suffer as a consequence of your separation may be intolerable to you.

You may envision their lives ruined, that they will be angry at you forever, and that you will carry this burden of guilt for the rest of your miserable life.

Column One: The Pied Piper Syndrome.

"I fear the terrible impact that bailing out will have on my children."

Column Two: Thoughts about the fear.

"I'll damage the children."
"I'll feel guilty forever."
"The children will be angry at me."
"I am evil for doing this to my children."

Column Three: Corrected perspectives.

• *It's highly likely that staying together would cause even greater upset to the children.* The fighting and the poor example of intimacy between my partner and myself will do a great deal of damage to the children, as well as provide them with a bad model of what marriage is like. Sometimes I have to trade short-term discomfort for the children—which no one doubts they will experience—to save them from possible long-term damage in terms of future problems with intimacy.

• *Children are amazingly resilient.* Generally, the permanent damage in relation to divorce occurs because the children weren't spoken to about the experience, or they were asked to choose sides, or the experience was one of the parents' constant fighting and complaining about each other. The act of bailing out in and of itself will not cause irreparable damage. It's how my partner and I behave during the process that matters. Also, if I let myself get too worried, the worry about how the children will manage will itself interfere with the amount of love, and the intensity and quality of the love and attention, I am able to provide the children during this difficult time.

• *I have not done this to hurt the children; therefore, I am not a malicious person.* I have rights and needs too. I have been a loving parent. I have built up a long history of love for, concern with, and attention to my children, and this one action does not change that at all. If I don't love myself, that is, if I don't take care of myself and address my own needs in relation to bailing out of this bad relationship, then what can I give to others? If I don't bail out, won't the children really suffer as a consequence?

• *Even if the children suffer, it is unlikely that the damage will be permanent.* Children who respond negatively to their parents' separation may appear to be having severely negative experiences, but they are often passing through what proves to be a transitory experience. As my home life comes back to normal, the difficult period will pass. (Later in this chapter and in chapter 6 we offer strategies and exercises to help you communicate with your children, help them express their fears and concerns, and help to make the bailing out experience as smooth as possible.)

• *If necessary, I can always get help to deal with my children.* There are numerous divorce and separation counseling services available to me through organizations, seminars, programs for children, therapists, and books. In the last fifteen or twenty years, there have been tremendous scientific strides in understanding how to help the children of separated or divorced parents. I am certainly not alone. There will be plenty of support if I need it.

• *I am unrealistic if I think my children are going to go through life without suffering any damage.* I must take a look at my own ideas about protecting them and my own unrealistic fantasies about how they *should* travel through life without ever being hurt or damaged or upset. While this is a disappointing and sad time for them, many millions of human beings have undergone this experience and have adjusted to it. It is possible that I am overdemanding of a predictable, safe environment for my children.

Column Four: Rate the beliefs in the corrected perspectives according to the list on the following page.

1 = disbelief ("I've written it down but I don't believe it at all.")

2 = intellectual belief and emotional disbelief ("I'm of two minds. I believe it intellectually, but I can't translate that belief into my feelings.")

3 = belief ("I have adopted this belief and made it my own. I have plenty of evidence to support it.")

Column Five: List experiences and exercises to help get over the fear and believe in the new perspectives on a gut level.

• **Speak with other men and women who have gone through this experience.** Educate myself on the subject. Read books and attend various programs and seminars offered by groups such as Parents Without Partners or my local church or synagogue that address the problem of how to deal with my children when I separate from my partner. I will accumulate overwhelming evidence that the children will survive.

• **I can utilize future projection (run a movie through my mind), imagining what life will be like two or six months later.** I can see my children coming back from a visit with their father. They are happy, not at all devastated, and they share with me that they are relieved that the tension is out of the air.

• **I can use the blowup technique to generate worst-possible scenarios built on my gravest fears.** When I immerse myself in these exaggerated images of my fears *and they are not* fulfilled, eventually my fear will be extinguished.

While you are encouraged to generate your own scenarios, here are some possible examples. Imagine the Society for the Prevention of Cruelty to Children picketing your home. Or imagine walking down the street and seeing your children standing on a soapbox, making speeches against you. A third might be that your children are in prison and they are pleading the cruelty of their parents as grounds for parole. A fourth example could take the visualization into a real-life action step, particularly if you are concerned about your reputation or your image if you do bail out. You could actually wear a button that reads, I Am a Cruel Mom. The key is that you actually do take the dreaded risk of exposing yourself and thereby attacking your shame. The button would naturally provoke questions and comments, and you could use these occasions as opportunities to share your fears and concerns about damaging your children if you bail out.

The following is another common fear we can run through the Fear Buster Chart. You might have exaggerated fears that you will damage your partner if you bail out. As a result, you will suffer the pangs of guilt forever.

Column One: The Ogre Syndrome.

"I'm afraid of hurting the other person."

Column Two: Thoughts about the fear.

"I'll feel terribly guilty about what I've done. It proves irrevocably what a despicable person I am."

"He's really tried hard. How can I do this to him? It's wrong to hurt someone who has tried so hard."

"Knowing that I've hurt him will cause me uncontrollable anxiety in the future. I won't be able to stop obsessing about this. I will be plagued with mental static about this forever."

"It's *always* wrong to hurt another person no matter what the circumstances."

Column Three: Corrected perspectives.

• *I should only feel guilty if I act maliciously, if I purposely set out to hurt another.* I should not feel guilty if I'm acting in my self-interest. Causing this person hurt proves nothing about me. It's his problem if he's feeling hurt by this, and while I can feel sympathy and compassion for his pain, it certainly does not prove anything significant about my being despicable. I certainly have not historically acted in a cruel fashion toward others. I've generally been a decent person. Guilt is a nonuseful emotion that doesn't belong here.

• *Just because he has tried hard to save our relationship doesn't relieve me of my responsibility to myself.* I've often tried hard in life and not always gotten what I wanted. The fact that he tried hard to make the relationship better is a commendable trait of his. I made every effort myself, but the bottom line is that if the chemistry isn't there or the feelings have died, then all this trying won't put the relationship back together again. If he ends up sad that the relationship breaks up, I shouldn't feel any guiltier because he tried.

• *It's highly unlikely that the thought that I've hurt him will remain in my mind indefinitely.* Like many other bad memories such as mourning someone who died, or financial losses, or personal humiliations, eventually the mental static ends. Anxiety is time limited. No one ever died from anxiety over bailing out, and there are numerous techniques for me to learn to control anxiey. Also, the anxiety is somewhat healthy in as much as it shows that my feelings of concern are real and not forced. I can use the anxiety as an opportunity to learn more effective ways of coping and getting on with my life. Some of the anxiety may also be useful in motivating me to move on.

• *Throughout my life, I've mistaken unassertiveness for politeness.* I was incorrectly taught to turn the other cheek, even when I was being hurt. I must use this as an opportunity to reject old teachings that have consistently gotten me into trouble. When my self-interest is at stake, frequently it is legitimate to stand up to another person and even to behave in ways that will ultimately lead that person to feel hurt.

Column Four: Rate the beliefs in the corrected perspectives as follows:

1 = disbelief ("I've written it down but I don't believe it at all.")
2 = intellectual belief and emotional disbelief ("I'm of two minds. I believe it intellectually, but I can't translate that belief into my feelings.")

3 = belief ("I have adopted this belief and made it my own. I have found plenty of evidence to support it.")

Column Five: List experiences and exercises to help get over the fear and believe in the new perspectives on a gut level.

• *Make a list and review all the things I've felt guilty about in the past year.* Ask myself honestly, has all the guilt I've felt led to anything constructive for myself?

• *Poll my friends about how despicable I am for bailing out.* I can write down (or record) the conversations, or I can repeat back to my friend what I *thought* I heard her say. Then I'll ask my friend if my interpretation of her statement is accurate. I should try to examine the *objective* results and then compare them with what I *thought* I heard. Honestly identify how your distort your friend's honest feedback, how you change the intent of that feedback. For example, you might ask a friend, "Listen, what do you honestly think about what I am going to do? This man loves me but I probably will hurt him. I feel very guilty." The friend might say something to you like, "Well, I couldn't do it myself. I admire you for doing it, but I couldn't see him suffering that much." You tend not to hear the comment "I admire you for it" and attend only to the remark, "I couldn't do it myself" and conclude from your misperception that decent people don't behave in such a manner.

• *Review the high and low points of my relationship in the last year or two, looking for malicious acts on my part.* Ask myself honestly, how much evidence is there for a continuing pattern of malice, or have most of my negative feelings and behavior resulted out of a growing sense of dislike or loss of love, and so forth? This review should prove once again that I am not purposely hurting the other person.

• *Find examples from my past, perhaps from my family life, where someone tried hard and I felt compelled to keep forgiving.* I might have sensitivities around this issue that are easily provoked.

For example, adult children of alcholics have historically been asked to forgive their parents over and over again. "Forgive your father for drinking. He's sick. He'll make it up to you." Ask yourself if you have developed this pattern of thinking that you *must* forgive and overlook when someone appears to be trying hard. Have you not been allowed to hold on to your rage and anger? Has your right to be angry been artificially taken away from you? You have the right to be angry, and you should let it motivate you to bail out.

• ***Run a movie in my head in which I announce to my partner that I am going to bail out.*** He begins to remind me of how he's been trying very hard. I see and hear him saying to me things such as "I've been in therapy," "I've tried very hard in therapy," "I got you all those gifts after you said I wasn't generous," and so on. In my visualization, I will see myself standing up to that. I will resist feeling guilty and resist feeling bad. I will feel strong and a powerful sense of self-esteem. I will see myself saying things to him such as, "I appreciate very much what you've done. You really have made an effort, but unfortunately, my feelings have just faded away and I can't feel good about the relationship any more. I simply can't renew my feelings for you."

• ***Assertively role-play with a friend.*** I'll ask a friend to pretend to be my partner trying to increase my guilt. My friend will say things such as "How can you do this to me?" "What am I going to do without you?" "I've done the very best I can." I will resist this onslaught and stand by my decision. The key here is that promises have been made before in the relationship many times and essential problems have still not been worked out. Ultimately, however, the relationship just didn't work.

In addition to the exercises you list in column five, choose any of the relaxation techniques described earlier and use them to reduce your feelings of anxiety. Systematic desensitization techniques are useful here as well. Rank order various situations that provoke the fear of hurting someone else and feeling guilty. Go through each item separately, imagining that fear realized. Use coping self-statements to reduce your anxiety. Follow the instructions given earlier in this chapter on systematic desensitization.

You might not be able to fill in all the columns in the Fear Buster Chart for all your fears provoked by the thought of bailing out on your own. The areas you are not able to complete or the fears you are unable to work with in the chart are probably areas in which a friend or perhaps a therapist could be of help. You could even work with the Fear Buster Chart in therapy sessions.

These fear busting techniques probably won't rid you *completely and totally* of the fears that keep you from bailing out, but they will help you gain enough control over them so that you can feel confident enough to begin to plan "how" you are going to bail out—to develop a strategy for ending the relationship that will make your landing as smooth and manageable as possible.

CHAPTER 6

How Do You Bail Out?

*T*he best time to leave is when you first realize that the relationship is not going to get better, when you know that "this is it." Nothing will change. If, like most people, you don't leave then, chances are you have embarked on the futile search for the right time. But the timing is never "right." You may offer excuses to yourself such as "I can't do it tomorrow because it's Easter" or "I can't do it next week because that's his first wife's birthday" or "I'm having my hair done" or "My son's getting braces." From the trivial to the mundane to the significant, it's a lifetime of special events. Never was Groundhog Day so important.

Ellen had wanted to leave her husband for a year, but just as she summoned up the courage to bail out, his father died. She decided to stay a while longer because it would be "too cruel" for her husband to lose his wife, child, and father at the same time. But three days after her father-in-law's death, Ellen was stricken with an agonizing ulcer attack that laid her low for four days. Despite her continuing misery, Ellen then decided she should graduate from college first because she didn't want to transfer to another college and lose credits when she returned to her parents' home in another state.

While waiting for another "right moment" to bail out, Ellen suffered a second ulcer attack. She remained in bed, immobile, for several days. Finally, Ellen made a tentative step: She consulted a lawyer, who mentioned that to get a divorce in that state, one party had to have been living there for three years. But Ellen was listening "selectively," and so she heard his statement to mean that both parties had to have been residents for three years.

Finally, despite her misconception of the residency requirement, Ellen decided not to wait until her third wedding anniversary (also "too cruel"). She bailed out a few months short of the imagined residency requirement.

Like many of you, some of Ellen's concerns were legitimate and some were not. But you must weigh these concerns against your own best interest. Was it worth Ellen's health and her personal pain to protect her husband? Instead of making those judgments, Ellen simply procrastinated in an automatic manner. Question the automaticity of your own decisions to delay bailing out. Note your tendency to view even minor issues as legitimate excuses for not acting.

The simple fact is that until you are ready, you are not going to act. Nothing can change that—not reading this book, not listening to your friends. What this book can do, however, is point out to you the opportunities to bail out, your self-defeating resistances to bailing out, and when you do bail out, help you to do so in the smoothest, most comfortable way possible.

If you have determined the time to bail out is long overdue, how do you actually do it? How do you just walk out? Do you call your dad, have a friend as witness, or call in the police? Do you disappear and leave a note? Or do you simply vanish?

Strategies for Bailing Out

Keep in mind that for most people bailing out is a slow, arduous process with many stops and starts. The thinking and behavioral changes may have been going on for a long time before the final, decisive leap. This is a necessary part of the process. The following are strategies people have used to help them make that final leap. Read them over and decide which would be appropriate for your own particular situation. Or you can plan your own course of action suited for your unique needs.

The Safety Net

The only way some people will bail out is to line up the next prospect and slide from the old relationship into the new one with a minimum of discomfort. In fact, sometimes a new relationship serves as the catalyst for leaving or for even considering bailing out.

Celia, a thirty-year-old commercial artist, was miserable in her relationship with a chronically depressed man. For three years, she agonized over whether or not to bail out. One weekend, Celia went to a convention and ran into an ex-lover. He flirted with her and asked her out. She accepted and he took her to an expensive restaurant for dinner and dancing. When Celia came to her therapy session, she told me, "I haven't felt like a woman in so many years, but I felt like Cinderella at the ball when he spent money and lavished attention on me. I didn't want to go back home. I didn't want the coach to turn into a pumpkin. For the first time in years, I felt a sense of hope, that there was a way out."

There was no doubt that this man could become Celia's safety net, and I did not discourage that in the therapy.

Gloria, a twenty-nine-year-old MBA who worked for a large company in New York, was married to a man who became increasingly troubled over the course of their eight-year marriage. While Gloria and her husband didn't fight, she had long outgrown the relationship and her husband's dependent behavior. Gloria's father had abandoned the family when she was six years old, so she was extremely sensitized to her child's need to have his father present. How could she possibly allow her son to feel abandoned in any way by his father? Gloria spent many sleepless nights engaging in mental fortune-telling, forecasting the horrible effects bailing out would have on her son.

Gloria connected with a man who was consulting in her company and began to lunch with him. At first, it was fairly innocent and the discussions primarily concerned business. But as it became clear that her relationship at home was deteriorating more and more, the meetings with her new friend became more heated and on a more personal basis. She told me she was trying to screen this new man for her child. Her husband would go out of town frequently, so she would find a way of getting together with her son and the man to discover how they responded to each other. That was the first hint I had that this man was being identified by Gloria as her safety net. After six to eight months, Gloria began to have an affair with her friend. The affair went on for about a year and a half, until, finally, through counseling, Gloria was able to bail out, assured that her son's needs would be taken care of. The affair then developed into a serious and loving experience.

Safety nets do sometimes go on to become primary relationships, but these relationships generally experience certain problems. Although Gloria and her safety net are still together, they do argue over promises that the safety net had made to her that were not fulfilled. One of the problems with safety nets is that because the partner is married or committed to another, the safety net thinks it's safe to make promises he may not be able to keep. Although they talk about it constantly, the safety net never truly imagines his lover will leave her relationship. Another reason safety nets may make promises that are hard if not impossible to keep is because most safety nets are rather compassionate, caring people. A person doesn't get scripted into that kind of role in somebody's life unless he has been identified as caring, warm, nurturing, and available. Unfortunately, these very attributes lead to promises that soothe at the moment but frequently can't be kept.

That, in fact, is what happened after Gloria's separation and divorce took place. She left a note for her husband and made the painful break. Her safety net was there, buying furniture for her new apartment and generally making life easier for her. But as their relationship wore on, things began to deteriorate somewhat because many of the promises were broken. The promises had to be broken. Many promises are not kept in this situation because they were made with the presumption that they would not have to be kept. Furthermore, a relationship in which one person is married is a high-tension, high-passion situation that carries with it a good deal of excitement. When that person is newly single, the bailer and the safety net settle in to becoming an ordinary couple. All the issues that befall all couples set in: boredom, routine, and the demise of the thrill of the chase. The excitement and electricity of the sequestered moments and stolen weekends are gone. She is totally available. He is totally available. All the problems that the safety net kept hidden from the bailer are now revealed: conflicts in their values and interests, secrets from the past, problems with his children, and so on. Because the clandestine phase of the relationship was conducted in the breathless excitement of continual crisis, neither had the time, the energy, or the inclination to talk about unpleasant and mundane issues. Before the breakup, the bailer and the safety net had to deal with The Problem: how to get her out of the relationship. Now that the crisis has resolved, the safety net transforms from a savior to a mere human being with clay feet.

For some people, it may not be appropriate to leapfrog from one relationship into another because they need time alone to discover what responsibility they had in turning the first relationship sour. They need to regroup themselves and work through the vestiges of anger and sadness associated with the past relationship. Without this period of self-reflection, they run the risk of simply repeating the same mistakes and creating more habitual negative patterns of thought and behavior.

Finding a safety net may not be the most appropriate solution for you. On the other hand, making new friends and developing new interests can serve as a kind of cushion that will diffuse your focus from the problem relationship and ease the transition from being part of a couple to beginning a new life on your own. As in every major transition in your life, it is important to have support. The support might be an understanding relative or friend, or you might seek the professional help of a counselor or therapist. Whatever your decision, you should designate in your mind exactly who that support person will be. Do not embark on the bailing-out process until you know exactly who that person is.

Should You Get a Therapist or Counselor to Help You Bail Out?

Many couples are afraid to leave because they don't want to live with regret. They say to themselves, "Look, I know deep down that this relationship isn't going to make it, but I have to go for counseling first." The counseling is designed less to rescue the marriage than to save them from their guilt. These people must believe that they have tried everything, that they have turned over every stone in their effort to save the relationship.

On the other hand, using the process of therapy or counseling to bail out is a reasonable choice for people who are somewhat cautious or risk adverse. The support of the therapeutic experience can ease the pain of separation. You are able to collect more and more data about your feelings and about strategies for making this change, and you buy more time to strengthen yourself for the future without your partner.

Should You Have a Trial Separation?

What is a trial separation and when do you need one? A trial separation is appropriate when you know you need space and you want to keep your options open. You're not absolutely convinced you want to bail out, but you are leaning strongly toward that decision. You need time and space to consolidate your choice. A trial separation provides an opportunity to reduce anger, backbiting, and hurtful and destructive arguments. In short, it is a cooling-off time. A separation also allows you to see what being alone feels like. It is an opportunity to gauge your feelings. This sense of freedom and separation you have been fantasizing about for several months or years is now real. If there are children, they also get a break from the tensions in the home.

What are the "rules" for a trial separation? The following suggested "rules" or guidelines are flexible and open to negotiation.

- You can either have no contact (that is, no telephone numbers or addresses are exchanged) or scheduled contact (regularly scheduled dates and calls).
- You can have no discussion of problems except in therapy or some limited, controlled discussion of problems. Some couples might spend fifteen minutes a day discussing problems; others do so only in the therapist's office. Still others might tape record their weekly discussions and bring them to the therapist. The agreements vary, but there must be some guidelines for discussing relationship problems.
- All "heated" discussions must take place under "on task rules." On task rules describe a strategy used in therapy to prevent discussions from degenerating into pointless bick-

ering. It is possible that these "rules" are foreign to you, but implementing them may lead to a new way of communicating that actually helps your relationship.

The following is a list of on task rules.

• *No "put-downs."* Name calling, sarcasm, and blaming are forbidden. Even if neither of you intends to put your partner down, if one person feels that she has been put down, that person has the right and obligation to tell the other party. Complaints should be voiced in terms of "I," such as "I had difficulty planning my leisure time because you did not let me know when you would be home" versus "You never let me know when you were coming home." If you are lodging a complaint, you should show a willingness to listen to your partner's point of view and accept his possible problems around the issue. You must demonstrate a willingness to cooperate in resolving the issue to both your satisfactions.

• *No "cutoffs."* Allow each other the time and space to state a position on a given problem. People hear but they often don't listen. That is, the sounds get through but the meaning is often lost because the "listener" is too busy formulating his rebuttal to pay attention to what the speaker is actually trying to communicate. In addition, if you interrupt, you are only receiving part of the information being communicated.

• *Do not answer one complaint with another.* "You never gave me gifts on my birthday" should not be answered by "Well, you never made the bed." All you get in such a discussion is a litany of problems, none of which is discussed, let alone ever resolved.

• *One problem at a time.* Keep the focus of your discussion on one issue. Avoid getting sidetracked by related but peripheral issues.

• *If one of you becomes emotionally upset, it is preferable to have that person withdraw from the discussion.* Do this only after the two of you have agreed on a time when the discussion will be resumed.

• *If either of you feels your message is not being communicated clearly to the other, for whatever reason, agree on how you will go about restating the message.* A good technique is for the listener to repeat what she *thought* she heard her partner say and for the speaker to check if his message got through clearly.

• *If one of you is asking for a change in behavior on the part of the other, make your request clearly and explicitly in terms of actual behavior.* It is futile and illegitimate to ask a partner to change feelings, to be "different" (to be more loving or less angry), or to make the vague request that your partner be more "understanding" of you.

Once a request for a change in behavior is made, the terms must be negotiated. How often must this changed behavior be exhibited? Where and when? An agreement must be worked out to the satisfaction of both partners. For example, a wife might request that her husband spend quality time with their children three times a week, reading to them, talking about problems at school and with friends, etc.

As part of the agreement, the person who is making the change in behavior should receive regular reinforcement from his partner to let him know that his efforts are appreciated.

If there is to be contact during the trial separation, specific, structured times and dates should be established for meetings and family outings. During the early stages at least, sexual contact should be prohibited, because lovemaking during the trial separation kicks off feelings of false security. The couple thinks everything is okay again, and the bad feelings are neutralized. As we know, however, the high is temporary. In addition, not having sex has the welcome benefit of taking pressure off both people. The woman does not have to fake pleasure, and the man does not have to perform as a great lover. Not engaging in sex also allows both parties to clarify their feelings. They see each other more objectively, and are able to make new resolutions about each other.

There must be a predetermined minimum length of time for the separation, generally three to six months. The terms can be renegotiated, either with the therapist or by the couple alone, to extend the time.

You must also set up certain criteria if you are to get back together. Those criteria might include items such as two months without any major fights, 50 percent increase in quality time spent with family, successful treatment in Alcoholics Anonymous, etc. *The simple passing of time is not enough. Criteria for reestablishing the relationship must be clearly established.*

Coping with the Volatile Partner

How do you deal with the irrational or volatile partner, and how do you separate from a violent person?

First, it is important to identify the thought patterns behind his irrationality. These cognitions frequently have to do with feelings of jealousy, abandonment, shame, humiliation, and failure. Look over your Fear Buster Chart to see if you can spot a fear you have that your partner may also be experiencing. This will help you understand your partner's behavior and better equip yourself to deal with it effectively.

It is important to note that although the vast majority of the threats that are made have no grounds, you cannot discount their importance. The following are some guidelines for dealing with the irrational or volatile partner.

• *To help the irrational partner, you should be aware that timing is everything.* There are good times and there are bad times to approach the subject of bailing out with a volatile partner. A good time is when the person's self-esteem is at a relative high, for example, after a promotion rather than after he's been fired. Be careful, however, not to use the issue of timing as an excuse to procrastinate.

• *It is important to talk about your pain within the relationship.* Try to avoid accusing the partner. Talk instead about the pain you are both experiencing, and how he deserves better in his life.

• *Speak to others who can influence your partner.* These could be parents or good friends. One woman was getting nowhere with a very volatile husband, so she told his good friend about the situation. The friend took the husband away for the weekend. By the time he returned, he had a new perspective on the relationship.

• *Gently point out his hypocrisy.* Tell him, "If you really love me and have concern for my welfare, you'll let me go."

• *Always hold out some hope with the volatile or disturbed partner.* Talk about trial separations, therapy, biding time, and possibly working things out in the future. All of the latter help to quell the savage breast.

• *At the same time, be clear and firm.* Don't send out confusing mixed messages. Don't say one thing and then contradict yourself the following day. These people need firmness. It's almost as if you are dealing with a child throwing a temper tantrum. He needs to know there are rules and that he cannot manipulate you through rage.

• *Try not to react with anger yourself.* Anger only sparks off more of the same in your partner, who will go even more out of control.

• *Again, the irrational or violent partner is a special case.* You might consider telling him of your decision to bail out in a public place so that he is less apt to create a scene or become violent. Make sure, however, that you have a place to go after he has been told.

• *Always remember, if there is real danger, you are justified in planning your departure without letting him know.* Arrange to have someone standing by to protect your physical well-being. Do not hesitate at any moment to call the police if necessary.

One woman had her father come pick her up, but she made the mistake of waiting until her husband came home to tell him she was leaving and taking their child. When the husband threatened her father, the police were called in. Even then, before she could make her exit, she had to promise to return in three days.

Coping with the Suicidal Partner

How do you deal with the suicidal partner? Much of the advice for coping with a volatile partner also applies to the suicidal partner, although there are some added components. First of all, it is important to note that many more people are blackmailed by suicide threats than by threats of violence. This is not to say suicide doesn't happen—it does. But it happens infrequently. And, if it does, you are certainly not the cause of it. If someone is going to commit suicide over the breakup of a relationship, you must assume that your partner's pain was a time bomb that was ticking away long before you met him. You just happened to be the one who triggered his long-standing decision.

People say they are going to kill themselves because either they incorrectly believe at the moment that they really mean it or they believe that they won't be able to tolerate the anticipated pain of separation. A third possibility is that they are trying to manipulate their partner. They know full well that they won't commit suicide. They are not really considering it, but they know historically that this threat will really affect their mate.

Here are some questions you should ask yourself to determine whether or not your partner is genuine in his threat to commit suicide.

• *Is there a plan?* Has he demonstrated that he has a well-thought-out, detailed strategy to do himself in? This is the single most important issue.

• *Is there a means?* Is there a weapon or does he have easy access to a weapon?

• *Has he put the plan and the means together?*

• *Has he exhibited changes in his personality recently?* These may include chronic depression, suspicious or paranoid thinking, or odd, out of character behavior. Another indication that the threat is real is if he is giving his belongings away to people. Does he seem to be closing the book on his life?

• *Is there a history of previous suicidal gestures or actual attempts?* Many individuals who ultimately commit suicide have a history of previous suicidal behavior.

• *Is he religious?* People who are religious may view taking their own life as a sin. Does he have certain important obligations in his life, such as the responsibility for caring for an aging parent or a child? People with these sorts of responsibilities are less likely to commit suicide.

• *Is he really without support—relatives or friends—or does he actually have plenty of support?* It might be helpful to make a list of his resources just to convince yourself that he's waxing dramatic and there's no real reason to believe he will carry out his threat.

If you go through that list and find that he is without support and there is a legitimate reason to believe he might attempt suicide, you should do the following:

Contact a therapist yourself.

Contact a suicide prevention organization in your community for advice and provide him with their resources.

Check up on him after you leave or ask someone close to look in on him often.

If possible, remove from the house any of the means he may have of hurting himself, for example, weapons or pills.

Contact his religious leader if there is one available.

If necessary, notify the police.

Seeing a therapist yourself may be the single most helpful act you can do, because in one session, you can describe the history of the relationship and what has happened since you revealed your intention to bail out. The therapist can help you judge the seriousness of your partner's threats and apprise you of the available resources and options. The therapist can also assist you in dealing with the emotional blackmail *you're* putting on *yourself*. That is, the therapist can help you realize how you are using your partner's threats to wallow in your own overblown guilt and sense of responsibility.

What Do You Tell the Children?

When you know you are bailing out, your children must be informed and given an opportunity within the home to talk through their feelings. You can schedule time with your child alone or with your partner. The key is to share with the child what is going on in as honest and candid a way as possible. Clearly, you have to modify your statements for younger and older children.

Techniques for Helping Children Bail Out

The truth is that you probably don't want to do a lot of cognitive work with preschool children in helping them to cope. They do much better with symbolic figures, such as dolls, puppets, and other concrete techniques such as role-playing. Sometimes older children can use visualization exercises successfully. As they grow, children pass through various phases of mental development. The abstract reasoning that is necessary for cognitive work is one of the last abilities to develop and, therefore, is appropriate for the older child only.

One of the authors left her husband when her son was two and a half years old, an age in which he did not have the abstract mental capacity to frame questions that could be answered by "intellectual," reasoned explanations. Eric never asked his mother a single question about why she had left his father, despite the fact that this occurred in a particularly dramatic manner. When the father would come to visit his son at the grandparents' house, he would barge through the door in an angry way, but the child still never asked a single question. By his father's third such visit, Eric had obviously drawn his own conclusions about how to cope with this uncomfortable situation. He greeted his father in a bright, phoney "social" voice and said, "Grandpa! (The grandfather was the coolest head in the home.) Guess who's here to see you! Why, it's Daddy! Daddy, say hello to Grandpa. Grandpa, say hello to Daddy!"

After yet another uncomfortable visit, Eric was riding in the car with his grandparents, a great aunt, and his mother. For half an hour straight, he queried each family member over and over: "Do you like Daddy?"

Unfortunately, his mother did not know what to do to help her son. She was, in effect, paralyzed by seeing her son's obvious pain. And she was unaware about how to broach the subject with such a young child. Because Eric hadn't asked any questions, she simply observed the same code of silence as her little boy.

The key is to somehow get the child to ask those questions and to talk about his feelings. How do you accomplish this?

Use drawings, puppets, or dolls. Frequently, court psychologists working with young children who cannot yet verbalize their thoughts and feelings engage youngsters in fantasy play. They have children make drawings or use puppets or dolls representing each parent as a way of getting children to communicate. This technique is often used, for example, to ascertain whether or not a child has been sexually abused or what is a child's preference in a custody battle. This kind of fantasy play can be very useful to you as a parent as well. Provide the necessary art supplies and some helpful coaching ("What does Daddy say to Mommy? What does Eric say?"). By observing your child's dramatic play, you will get valuable insight into what's going on. Then, using the same play, you can reenact the same situations but with revised, "happy" endings that are

in line with reality but also represent a comfortable resolution
for the child. For example, the child goes off with mommy
and lives happily with daddy visiting occasionally. Or the
child does things with mommy and also does things with
daddy.

Try visualization. The visualization experiences you employ
should mimic and incorporate what the child is likely to feel
rather than provide unrealistic images that avoid any discomfort. These visualizations should also incorporate reassurances
from the parents and coping self-statements that the child can
learn to feed himself during his day-to-day experience. Remember, the point is to have the child express his feelings, his
conflicts, and, most important, his fears. After the child ex-
presses his feelings, the same elements are used to reassure him.
For example, the following is an exercise you might use for a
young child who is terrified by the prospect of visiting his dad
and the dad's girlfriend in the new setting. Have him relax in
a chair or on the floor or a bed. Sit close to him. Ask him to
close his eyes and visualize a scene: Guide him through the
scenario where he is visiting his dad. Tell him, "You are having
dinner at dad's new house. You are feeling scared and uncomfortable." Then introduce an alternative cognition. Have the child
tell himself, "This is a natural feeling. Sure, I should feel a
bit strange. I haven't had this experience before, but each time
I visit my dad in his new home, it will get easier and easier."
If appropriate, he can also tell himself, "I know Dad loves me,
and I'm happy that a lot of the bad feelings between my parents
are gone. Life will be easier without bad feelings in my home."

Or the child can visualize dealing with teasing peers. School-
mates have heard that his parents have separated and are
teasing him about it. The child visualizes himself coping
with the teasing, making appropriate responses such as explaining that his parents didn't get along, that many people get
divorces these days, and that he is kind of relieved that his
parents have resolved the situation this way so he doesn't have
to witness their arguing and pain anymore.

Another visualization might involve saying good-bye to a parent when the weekend is over. The child feels sad; he might even be crying. But he copes by feeding himself self-statements that remind him that he will get used to this situation: "Of course, I feel bad, but the weekend was wonderful and I know my dad loves me." Or "I'll see him in two weeks."

Role-playing is another technique. You can have the younger child express his feelings to you as both of you pretend to be someone else, such as the big bear and the little bear. The little bear's daddy has just gone off into the forest and may not be back for some time. What does the little bear say? This role-playing incorporates a kind of fable.

The key in helping your child is to be aware that children, particularly the younger ones, engage in a great deal of magical thinking in which they blame themselves for the separation. The parents' goal, therefore, is to help the child not blame himself in any way. This raises an interesting dilemma. Parents will often tell their child, "One of the reasons we are splitting up, honey, is because we don't want to keep fighting and hurt you." Now, that may be true. One of the reasons you may be splitting up is because you see the negative effects of the relationship on the children. The problem is that the very young child may magically interpret that as "They are splitting up to save me." So, you have to be very careful and weigh your statements in terms of what is appropriate for your child's age. Older teenagers can understand that such a statement shows love and concern, but younger children are likely to misinterpret the statement and blame themselves. In a similar way, children feel a terrible burden if they think their parents stayed together because of them yet are miserable as a couple and hate each other. The postdivorce child does much better when he sees a rational model of parents attacking problems.

Older children can role-play all sorts of situations, such as explaining the divorce to friends, or visiting father in his new home for the first time. The child simply role-plays himself and the person who is playing with him assumes different roles, such as the friends or the father. The goal is to help the child get in touch with his feelings and to talk about them. Another type of role-playing has two children interacting with each other. One of my patients knew another woman who was also going through a divorce. The mothers put the children together and let them play different parts. The children even played mother and father as the mothers assisted the children in explaining to each other why the parents weren't feeling like friends anymore.

Mary, a preteenager, was having difficulty dealing with her new stepfather. She felt abandoned by her real father and was enraged that this new person was taking his place, even asking her to call him "daddy." A counselor at school played the role of her stepfather. He encouraged her to express her feelings and also to express compassion for the stepfather's situation. He had her say something like, "I understand, Joe, that it must be terrible for you to come into a family and take over as a father. I understand how difficult it must be for you, but you have to understand how angry and disappointed I am that this has happened."

As children get older, they also experience another profound set of fears. According to Judith Wallerstein, one of the authors of *Second Chances*, they become increasingly afraid that they are going to repeat the mistakes that their parents made when they grow up. They become afraid to expect love; they hope for it, but certainly do not ever let themselves feel entitled to it. One of the most important goals, then, is to change their idea that because it happened to their parents (the disappointment and problems that eventuated in their parents' splitting), it must happen to them. Parents must help their children capture something good from the memories of their parents' marriage and not involve them in their continuing anger.

The following is a sample dialogue between a parent and

her ten year old. It can serve as a guide for your own discussion with your children:

> PARENT: I've got to tell you something that is really uncomfortable for me to talk about, but because Daddy and I love you so much and respect your intelligence, we have to tell you. We have stopped being the kind of friends that we used to be, so we are going to live apart. Remember when you broke off with your friend, Timmy? You hurt so much and thought that you two were so different that you couldn't get back together again?
>
> CHILD: But who will I live with? (Children are notoriously caught up with their own issues, often ones we couldn't have anticipated, such as "Who will give me Christmas presents?" "Who will I live with?" "Who will take me to Little League?" and so on.)
>
> PARENT: Because we both love you, you will share your time with both of us, and we will work out a plan.

As the dialogue continues, allow the child to ask all his questions, no matter how trivial or irrelevant they might appear from your adult point of view. Be sure to distinguish between the nature of the relationship between you and your partner and the bond shared by each of you with your child. Assure the child that the diminishment of feelings or the break in friendship between you and your partner is not something that will happen between either of you and your child. For example:

> PARENT: You are the person we both love the most. We both want to continue taking care of you and being friends with you. You are my child and that's something that never changes. I'll never stop loving you even if you did many, many things that hurt and disappointed me. (You may cite some examples here where the child disappointed you, but you continued to love him.)

One couple played for their children a tape that recorded the parents discussing their separation. The parents related on tape how much they loved their children and that they did not want to continue the fighting that could only hurt the children more. These parents needed to put the discussion on tape because they felt it was too difficult to be candid and open in front of the children. They also needed to hear how the discussion sounded before presenting it to the children, so that they could make any modifications. Listening to the tape with their parents present gave the children a chance to comment and ask questions. It was an opportunity to understand and integrate the information.

Again, it is important to keep in mind that children often think that if their parents can stop loving each other, then they can stop loving their children. It is essential to assure children that nothing could be further from the truth. In fact, parents should be reassured themselves that it is likely that as they stop loving each other, there's more energy, more interest, and more love available for the children. What you must avoid is a conspiracy of silence. You don't want the children to go off into their rooms and not talk about their fears and concerns. You don't want them to talk *only* to their friends about the situation and get all sorts of misinformation, although sharing their fears with their friends can be helpful. You want them to talk to you first about what they are feeling.

When you talk to your children, there are a variety of techniques you can employ to get your child to talk about what he is feeling and to share what the experience is like for him. For example, you can have your child complete sentences out loud, such as the following:

"When I think about Mommy and Daddy living apart, I _____."

"Even though Mommy and Daddy tell me it's not my fault, I still feel _____."

Perhaps you can think of other sentences that are more appropriate to your own situation.

What About Family and Friends?

What do you tell parents and friends? How can they help you to bail out smoothly?

Before you approach your family and friends, consider the following list of fears commonly experienced by people who are about to bail out. Check the ones that apply to you.

____ My parents and friends won't be supportive.

____ My parents and friends will humiliate me.

____ My parents and friends will say, "I told you so."

____ My parents and friends will secretly be happy at my pain.

Add your own fears to this list.

Now, look over the fears you checked and/or added to the list and ask yourself, "How realistic are these fears?" Then ask yourself, "What exact role do I want my family and/or friends to play in my bailing out? How can they be helpful?"

Create a "Bailing Out Support Chart" to clarify this issue. Take a large sheet of paper or oaktag and divide it into four columns, from left to right. Use the following outline to fill in the chart.

Column One: Name of person.

Column Two: How can she be helpful?

Moral support and advice
Legal or counseling help
Financial support
Contacts for housing, jobs, etc.
Mediation with spouse/partner

Add any other areas of help and support you can think of.

Column Three: What self-defeating or interfering cognitions do I have about using this person in this role? (These can be drawn from your list of fears and from the list in column two.) Here are some examples.

She'll say, "I told you so."
She'll be secretly happy at my pain.
I don't want him to know how little money I have.
He'll use it against me.
If he does me a favor now, I'll be forever indebted to him.

Add your own fears to this list.

Column Four: Evidence of the falseness of these interfering cognitions. Try to come up with reasons why your fears are unfounded and write them in this column. For example:

He's always been supportive of me. Why should he change now?
Is there any reason to believe that he is secretly glad this is happening to me? Hasn't he given me every evidence that he is concerned about this situation?
When I've borrowed money from him in the past, has he really held it up to me? Has he really made me squirm?

When you do sit down to tell parents, other family members, and friends, your goal should be to be as straightforward as possible about what has happened. In some cases, you can confide the details; in other cases a simple explanation will suffice: "Listen, we just have fallen out of love." The key to determining what to say is to gauge who your audience is and the level of intimacy you share with that person.

The Mechanics of Bailing Out

How do you actually bail out? Should you write a letter explaining why you want to bail out as an initial step? If you do decide to write a letter first, should you be absent or present when he reads it? Should you offer him a chance to respond? How extended should your discussions be about separating? Should you leave a note and then walk out the door?

Different situations require different behaviors. Writing a letter to someone and talking about the problem are genuinely different. If you attempt to explain your reasons for bailing out in person, he is likely to offer counterarguments. Either you become embroiled in another pointless conflict, or your resolve can be weakened. Also, oral words are temporary, but written words are permanent and, therefore, have more weight.

A patient once told me that she went away for a week, leaving her husband a long letter that detailed her sadness and pain. When she returned, he told her that he felt what she was saying more deeply than he had ever experienced in any of their conversations. Sitting down with that letter, reviewing it, staring at it, and knowing his wife had written these words was very powerful for him. Because he was finally able to comprehend her reasons for bailing out, he was able to accept the split without acrimony.

You also have to ask yourself how you have handled these difficult situations before. Have you two talked about your problems before? Does he get wild when you confront him on various issues? If you tell him you want to bail out, what's the likelihood of his becoming violent?

When we are bailing out, most of us need to clarify our position fully to our partner. We need to give that final explanation, make that final statement. Sometimes we may even want to give that extra twist of the knife. Whatever our reasons, this is the time when we want to express what we haven't really expressed in all those years. But sometimes we can't express it all, either in notes or through talking. Some things must remain unexpressed. Can you accept a lack of absolute certainty that he understands every possible nuance of why you are bailing out?

If you do write a letter, it should contain *some* of the following points:

• The letter should express in simple terms your regrets about what has happened. It shouldn't be long and convoluted, but straightforward.

- It should explain why it seems necessary to you to bail out.
- It should state why it will be better for all concerned, including him.
- It should contain a reminder of the good times in an attempt to salvage his self-esteem.
- If you wish, some statement of hope for the future might be included. This depends on how absolute you are in your decision to bail out.
- It should attempt to allay his particular fear(s). When you bail out, your partner generally has some particular anger or fear relating to you. He may be jealous or suspicious that you are involved with someone else, or paranoid that you've told his family about him. Try to assuage that fear.
- Finally, the letter should include a firm review of the rules of the separation and your expectations during the breakup, including:

Whether or not you want to have any contact with him
What you will do about money
How you will handle mutual friends
How you will handle already planned engagements, such as
     weddings, etc.

Whether or not you are present when your partner reads your letter and whether or not you offer him a chance to respond depends entirely on your history together. If during confrontations in the past, he has been sane and able to talk things through, fine. But if there's any evidence that discussions will simply degenerate into accusations and counteraccusations, then there should be no chance offered and you should just leave.

Communication Skills Necessary for Bailing Out

• When you do express your feelings in a discussion with your partner, stick to sentences that begin with "I feel" rather than "you" statements that are accusatory and judgmental and only cause your partner to become defensive and hostile. For example, "I feel unhappy" is preferable to "You make me unhappy."

• Be balanced in your explanation. Mention qualities about your partner that you respect and like, before you detail the unsolvable difficulties that have led to your decision to bail out. For example, "As I've told you many times before, I admire greatly your commitment to your work and your extraordinary ability to be patient with your family and some of my friends. These are some of the things I've enjoyed immensely about you. However, there are irreconcilable problems having to do with your lack of attention to me and your lack of commitment to our relationship that I can no longer abide."

• If your partner refuses to understand or accept your decision, you are not responsible to stick in there until he finally understands. That, in all probability, will never happen. Simply repeat your "I feel" statements until you realize you can't go any further.

• Be clear and firm in the expression of your decision to bail out. Many people in this situation send mixed messages. They confuse their partner. More than ever before, your partner needs a firm clarification of your position. At this point, you can't be fuzzy, wimpy, or load your explanations with qualifications such as "If only you would change, I could see myself living with you."

• Remember, you are not responsible for how your partner responds to your decision to bail out. You can express empathy, but do not assume responsibility for his pain. For example, "I understand your pain. It reminds me of the pain I suffered when George left me six years ago. I also know, just as I know it from myself, that you'll get through this. It'll take time, but you've gotten through difficult crises in our relationship before, and you'll get through this one. You're a survivor and you always land on your feet.''

Preparing for the Single Life

Preparing for the single life ahead of time can reassure your fears about being alone. You know you will be okay after you bail out, so you are, therefore, more motivated to take that leap. How can you prepare yourself for the single life while you're still in the relationship? Here are some areas to consider.

• *Overcoming your fear of being alone.* First, review your Fear Buster Chart in chapter 5. Identify the exact fear you are experiencing. A common fear is the Robinson Crusoe Syndrome. Go through all the columns of the chart. Review the exercises. If necessary, do them over again.

Second, you must spend time alone. Sit down with other men and women who have spent time alone. Ask them what their experience has been like. What was the most difficult time? Plan a series of events that will distract and engage you while you are spending time alone. Review some of the solitary activities you've enjoyed in the past. When you were a child you spent numerous hours alone. It's only now that you are an adult that you've forgotten how to entertain yourself *by yourself.* You can go to the movies, play solitaire, listen to music, work on a neglected hobby, keep a diary, or add to your miserable memories list (see chapter 7 for details on how to create a miserable memories list). Even watching television has been found to be very helpful during this period.

Finding new interests and friends is much more difficult than renewing interests and old friendships. People are creatures of habit. If you were told to go out and find new friends and new interests, it is unlikely you would do it. Create a list of all the activities you have found interesting, pleasurable, or have mastered at some point in your life: golf, tennis, cartooning, collecting coins, looking at real estate, etc. The list should include at least thirty or forty items. Identify three activities that you will pledge to take up again. When you became a couple, you may have dropped many activities you pursued as a single person. Commit yourself to renew some of those old interests.

You may be embarrassed to call old friends you neglected when you were with your partner because they might say, ''I told you so,'' or because you neglected them for so long. You might feel guilty about your disloyalty. Challenge that fear. If you had a friendship with someone earlier, there is every reason to believe you still have something in common.

- *Deciding on and preparing future living arrangements.* First, list your particular needs. What are your primary concerns in terms of space, convenience, roommates for company, geographical accessibility to your friends, and type of neighborhood? Everyone has his own idiosyncratic needs, so it's important to think first about what will make you happy.

Second, think about any irrational cognitions you are having concerning a drop in your standard of living. That is a common concern of both men and women because both partners frequently suffer a drop in standard of living. Take a look at that fear and run it through the Fear Buster Chart described in chapter 5.

On a more practical level you should do the following:

Register with a broker.

Find out which friends want roommates.

Discriminate between temporary living arrangements and a permanent home. It's fine to live with a friend while you think things over. From there you can plan a more permanent residence.

Some people return to their parents' home. That solution has its pros and cons. It's quick and convenient, and usually they are waiting with open arms. On the other hand, it's another reminder of failure and that you can't

handle things independently. You're also likely to be
exposed to their slings and arrows. It's a trade-off. Consider that alternative carefully.

• **_Preparing a smooth transition for the children._** Review
the section earlier in this chapter on children for guidance in
helping your children express their concerns so that you can
give them the appropriate reassurances.

Prepare your child for what it will be like when the other
parent is no longer there. Will there be a change in his room?
If that parent had a study or his own bedroom, the child will
want to know who or what will take the parent's place. Or
who will sleep in the bed with you? The child will want to
know about changes in friends and in his school situation. It is
essential that you speak with the school guidance counselor
and his teacher about the situation and your child's particular
needs. Ask if the teacher or counselor can arrange to have
your child spend a little more time with children of other
single parents. The most frequently reported reaction of children in this situation is a feeling of "oddness," of being
"strange" without the other parent. "I felt I was different
than the other kids," is a common remark. You need to give
your child exposure to other children of single parents to
reassure him that he is not the only one in this situation.

You can also review books on separation and check out
Parents Without Partners for tips on how to deal with children
who are either moving to a new home or having one parent
move from the family home.

If you are going to move, tell the child exactly what moving
day will be like. Take your child to the new home before
moving day. Walk around the new neighborhood and familiar-
ize the child with the house, the streets, and, if possible, with
new neighbors. Make it an adventure. Include a treat, such as
ice cream, to help the child begin to associate the new environment with something rewarding. If you have access to the
new home before moving day, show the child where his room
will be. Allow the child an appropriate amount of participation

in decorating it. This is also an opportunity to talk about visitation, and to ask the child whether or not he wants to provide any input. As a result, the child will have more of a sense of control over the process.

As much as is appropriate to his age, let the child participate in packing his things on moving day. Don't wince if he wants to have a picture of daddy. The child needs as smooth a sense of continuity as possible.

• *Know the divorce laws* **before** *you bail out from a marriage.* This is the best guarantee of an equitable future settlement. Many books are published and seminars conducted on the mechanics and legalities of divorce. Perhaps the most effective way of getting the information you need is to network with other divorced people to learn about the educational, counseling, and legal programs available to you.

If you are married, find a lawyer before you bail out. It is advisable to go for a consultation, even if it has to be on the sly. It's also a good idea to consider divorce mediators. Divorce mediation, that is, using a counselor or psychologist who works along with the lawyer, is a much less expensive, cumbersome way of getting through the process. If successful, you and your partner will arrive at an amiable agreement that precludes time-consuming and costly litigation in court.

CHAPTER 7

What Can You Expect When It's Over?

The Steps to Adjustment after Bailing Out

What can you expect from a good adjustment? Just as there are specific steps to quitting smoking or grieving over the death of a loved one, there are steps or stages you can expect to go through after you bail out. Not only can you expect to run through the gamut of human emotion but emotional highs often give way suddenly, almost without warning, to emotional lows.

While these steps are presented here as distinct and sequential, in reality, they tend to overlap. You may skip one step altogether, pass through another quickly, stay stuck in yet another for months at a time, or you may pass out of a stage only to return to it some time later. Whatever your individual experience, you should be prepared to go through the following stages and steps.

• *Numbness.* If you have not been exposed to any dramatic abuse or dramatic behaviors on the part of your partner, if it's been more a matter of a gradual disintegration of loving feelings, you may experience a numbness that is much more powerful than if you have undergone dramatic abuse. You might say things to yourself such as "I'm not sure I'm really doing this." "It feels like a bad dream." "I'm bailing out, but I'm not sure I can go through with it." "I'm too afraid to turn back, but did I do the right thing?" "I'm a little bit ashamed to back out since I've made this public, but I'm not really sure I should bail out. On the other hand, I'll really feel terrible if I do back off and let myself down."

These thoughts can lead to a kind of mental paralysis. You may move through this early stage in a dreamlike state. You've made the decision, either with a therapist, a lawyer, a good friend, or on your own, but you're numb, disconnected from your feelings. In a way, that's how the body and the mind react to protect you through a crisis, whether it's a trauma such as getting mugged or being in a car accident or bailing out of an aircraft or a relationship. You go forward, you act, but at this point, you lack real conviction.

Caroline, who had been separated for two weeks, reported that every day after work she would experience a "dreamlike feeling." She would say to herself, "Maybe if I pinch myself, I'll wake up."

• **Fear.** The first night alone is the best example of this stage. You're in bed by yourself, and you begin to feel an absolute terror, along with a sense of detachment and anxiety. The feeling can take on various dimensions, but the bottom-line emotion is fear.

About three months after bailing out, Claire had thought she was doing very well. Then one day, she received the divorce agreement in the mail and she came to me reporting a full-blown panic attack. She was continually hyperventilating and experiencing heart palpitations, uncontrolled sweating, and racing and pressured thoughts. In serious cases, these fearful feelings can lead to the development of phobias, panic disorders, obsessive worrying, even nervous tics or habits or an increase in addictive behavior. Therefore, the beginning signs of fear must be attended to immediately. Use the Fear Buster

Chart in chapter 5, do your relaxation exercises, seek out counseling, or even, if necessary, see your doctor and undergo a short-term course of tranquilizers or antidepressants. It is important, however, to work on these initial symptoms right away because they are generally very circumscribed and can be controlled at this early stage.

• *Regret.* "What have I done?" you ask yourself. "Did I make a mistake?" You become a Monday-morning quarterback, replaying your actions and looking for the fatal mistakes. This is a good time to go over the lists and self-tests that provide the "evidence" you need in support of your decision. If you are lucky, someone who cares about you will talk you out of your regret. Your friend will remind you of the very good reasons why you bailed out and reassure you that you made the right decision.

Cognitive dissonance is a notion in psychology that refers to how difficult it is to be comfortable once you've made a decision. For example, if a person can't decide whether to buy a Ford or a Chevy, and finally chooses the Ford, he will tend to spend a good deal of time obsessing about all the wonderful attributes of the Chevy. This is called "postdecision rumination" and is really a universal phenomenon. The alternative you did not choose frequently takes on a greater value in your mind and contributes to feelings of regret. Of course, this phenomenon is very common when people bail out. The ex-partner is seen in the rosy afterhaze of the breakup and becomes an object of obsessive, regretful thoughts.

A month after her bailout, Pauline was full of regret about her decision. To hear her speak, it was as if she had left the most wonderful man in the world. She had received a great deal of support during the bailing-out process from a girlfriend. Then the friend had gone to Europe for a month, thinking Pauline would be fine. But left on her own, Pauline was flooded with regrets. During her therapy with me, we constructed a miserable memory list (described later in this chapter), did relaxation training, and did a good deal of cognitive restructuring. Essentially, we followed the program outlined in this book. Pauline soon regained a clearer perspective.

• *Sadness.* You will inevitably pass through a stage of sadness accompanied by resignation and acceptance. "Why didn't it work?" you ask yourself. "It's too bad it didn't work out. I know I can't go back. I know it's the right decision, but a part of my life is cut out forever. The dreams, the hopes, the history we were going to establish with each other are shattered and gone." This is similar to the sadness we experience when we mourn the death of a loved one. A key difference, of course, is that bailing out is not as final.

Almost immediately after bailing out, Laura would frequently cry spontaneously, think morbid thoughts, and even contemplate suicide. She was overwhelmed by sadness about certain aspirations she had set for herself and her partner. Laura had grown up in an environment in which everything her demanding, high-achieving parents would plan invariably materialized. Laura had focused on certain goals for the relationship and was overwhelmed by sadness that these goals had not been reached.

As she learned to change her habitual thought patterns through the techniques outlined in this book, Laura became more flexible in her thinking. She came to recognize that her life presented all sorts of other opportunities and alternatives. Even though the end of this relationship was sad and disappointing, she recognized that her goals in a relationship did not *have* to be met by this particular man.

• *Rage.* Rage follows close on the heels of sadness, and you may likely find yourself Ping-Ponging back and forth between the two emotions. Rage is characterized by self-statements such as "Why did he wreck my life?" "Why did he wreck me?" "How could I let him do this to me? How could I have let myself down so?" "Why has God made people like this?" "What a son of a bitch to hurt me the way he did!" "Why didn't he come clean right away with these crazy ways of his? Why did he wait until I was so in love with him and had spent so much time with him?"

Once Laura felt less sad about the end of her relationship, she became full of anger at the ex. The anger actually manifested itself in the form of some anonymous calls to his employer during which she would say things such as, "Did you know that he's been pilfering materials from the storeroom?" She was thoroughly embarrassed about these calls but felt that she couldn't control her need to make them.

Laura came to realize that although it would have been nice if he were different, there was no rule that said he *should* have understood her better or that he *should* have helped her achieve their goals. Once she accepted the fact that her bad relationship was an unfortunate experience but that she could survive without it, her rage finally dissipated, as had her sadness.

• *Acceptance and freedom.* In this, the final stage, you recognize that the breakup was for the best. You review all the reasons you bailed out, but the review here is not so much to mourn but to justify the decision. You now have thoughts such as, "It was the right decision. I'm glad I made it." "I'm pleased I can now get on with my life." "All kinds of opportunities are now open to me socially and romantically." "I'm no longer inhibited and blocked as I was within the relationship."

Laura did eventually recognize that the breakup was for the best. She had gone through all the previous stages. I kept reminding her that she would reach this stage, but she had always denied the possibility. She was absolutely convinced she would be stuck in one of the other stages. One day, she reported feeling freer, as if a tremendous burden had been lifted from her shoulders. She actually reported to me, "I can finally feel free again at work [where she had been having a terrible time concentrating] and I can reach my potential." Two months after she made that statement to me, she got an important promotion and a raise.

How to Smooth Your Way

Create a Ritual

The first thing you need to do to make a good adjustment after you have bailed out is to somehow ritualize the breakup. Just as you have a ceremony to commemorate the occasion of a marriage, as well as other important life transitions, I believe you also need some kind of ceremony to mark when you said good-bye. This can be as simple as getting together with friends and laughing about your good fortune, reviewing the reasons about why you bailed out, and making up funny poems and limericks about why you split—the cornier the better. One woman wrote, "There once was a young woman from Queens / When it came to love she didn't know beans / Her main man was Tom / Oh! What a bomb! / She dumped him and ended the scenes." The idea is to create an occasion that helps you put a punctuation mark at the end of the relationship. Using humor or levity is certainly a good way of doing that. Generally, the best people to celebrate with are friends rather than family. These friends have shared the ups and downs. They have been your confidantes and know what you have gone through.

Marie was a cartoonist. When she ended her relationship, she invited friends over for a cartooning party. She drew some funny cartoons about the rise and fall of her relationship and shared them with her friends. Then they all played a version of the game called "Pictionary," in which they drew pictures of different aspects of her relationship and then guessed what each drawing represented. The friends drew pictures of Marie and her ex arguing, of a time when the boyfriend had broken his nose, and so on. They had a merry old time rollicking about it.

After the party, Marie reported to me how much better she felt. It was the first time in a long time she had actually been able to get a good perspective on the relationship and realize that bailing out was the best thing she could have done for herself.

Distract Yourself

Another simple technique to help you over the rough spots is simply to distract yourself. Indulge in one of the pleasures you rediscovered in the Fear Buster Chart (chapter 5) under column five and in the list you compiled to rediscover old friends and activities in chapter 6.

After she bailed out, Sonya revived her old interest in horseback riding. For years, she had felt restricted about riding because her boyfriend was not a rider. He used to worry about Sonya hurting herself, and she had also detected that he was somewhat jealous of the owner of the stable. Now, whenever she felt lonely or depressed, Sonya went riding.

Take a Vacation

If it is at all possible, taking a vacation is a good choice. In new surroundings, away from the triggers (people, places, lifestyle habits, and objects) that remind you of your ex, you'll be more open to meeting new friends and to feeling good.

After bailing out of her marriage, Marlene remained in the same home she had shared with her ex-husband, Brian. She found it difficult to be in an environment so closely associated with him, so she took a two-week vacation to the Caribbean. The vacation spot, so different from her home, provided a welcome break. She had the time to be by herself in a new place and to adjust to the separation. When she returned to her home, it was as if she had created a bridge between her former life with Brian and her new life as a single woman.

A vacation is another type of ritual, almost like a honeymoon at the end of a relationship. It's also a good idea to get out of town if you are receiving a flood of "begging" calls or visits

from your ex. Persistent pleas to win you back can effectively
erode your determination, particularly if you are going through
your own bouts of regrets, guilt, sadness, and loneliness.
Being inaccessible can be your best countermeasure to his
pursuit.

Be with Friends

Being with close friends who understand and care about
you can be a great source of comfort.

Susan's best friend lived in another part of the country, so
Susan arranged for her friend to come stay with her for the
first crucial weeks after she bailed out. Her friend's visit
provided a helpful transition from her life as a couple to her
life as a single person. This is not a time to hide your feelings
or feel ashamed of your needs. The company of a good friend
can be the most soothing balm to your initial emotional turmoil. If it is impossible to have a friend stay with you, do not
hesitate to ask friends to set aside a certain amount of time for
you, so that you know during those periods you will not be
alone.

Coping with Second Thoughts

Second thoughts that tempt you to make that fateful telephone
call can be understood in terms of a phenomenon extensively
researched by experts in alcoholism. It's called "the abstinence violation effect" and originally was conceived of by Dr.
Alan Marlatt. When the recovering alcoholic slips, he generally has engaged in what is called "an apparently irrelevant
decision" (AID), a decision that seems irrelevant to violating
abstinence at the time it is made but often leads to a bout of
drinking. For example, an unknowing dinner guest brings the

recovering alcoholic host a bottle of wine. Then, after the guests leave, the alcoholic finishes off the bottle, thereby ending a lengthy period of abstinence.

A similar cycle is often reenacted by a person who has bailed out. Francine was out of her relationship for more than a year. She no longer thought much about her ex-partner. She had no trouble abstaining from calling him, although during the early months she had felt compelled to call him quite frequently. But a year later, she carelessly decided to contact a friend who was also close to her ex. They had dinner together and, of course, spent the entire evening discussing the ex-lover. The next morning she was unable to keep from making that phone call.

This is how the abstinence violation effect works. The first step is the apparently irrelevant decision that ultimately leads to violating the abstinence. When the alcoholic slips and goes from one drink into a binge, it is usually because he starts condemning himself for that initial slip. He feels hopeless about having taken that first drink. The dam has burst, the water has flooded, and he's lost. This can be applied to bailing out. When you begin to have second thoughts, you condemn yourself for your "weakness." Those self-condemning thoughts unleash a flood of regrets that make you feel worthless. They lead to such self-talk as, "I'd better hold on to this person because no one else is going to want me." You must interrupt that process.

You can learn how to short circuit those feelings of loneliness and second thoughts by not condemning yourself for having these thoughts in the first place. Second thoughts are normal. It's appropriate to miss somebody with whom you've been involved, someone with whom you've been sexually intimate but who you've decided is either too destructive for you or just not appropriate. Second thoughts often take the following forms.

• *"He was so good to me and for me."* There's a tendency to review all the good things the partner did and not to remember the bad things. When I ask patients to review the relationship they just bailed out of, they frequently will remember only the positive.

When Joan had been bailed out for five months, she began to express the thought that "he was the only man who made me feel sexually alive," and that no one she had met could begin to measure up to him. She was forgetting all the reasons she had for leaving. When I reminded her that their sexual experiences were the *only* bright spot in the relationship and that most of the time out of bed she was miserable and fearful, she was shocked at how easily she had forgotten her unhappiness. Once she remembered all aspects of the relationship, she was able to put her sexual needs in perspective.

• *"Others live with difficult people. Why couldn't I?"* There's an implicit self-denigration in that thought: "Others have been able to tolerate unmanageable people. There must be something wrong with me that I wasn't able to handle this person. Maybe it was me." This is just an old, repeated pattern.

Sandra became very self-condemning about a year and a half after bailing out. She expressed great regrets about her decision. The primary focus of her regret was that she observed a number of her friends who were involved with very difficult men and wondered why she couldn't tolerate it as they did. I challenged her belief with the following statement: Others live miserably with miserable people. Perhaps on the surface, it appears they are tolerating it, but frequently they are just as unhappy as you were. Also, as we get healthier, we are attracted to healthier people. You should be pleased that you are going out with healthier people. Where is it written that you have to have the patience of Job, that you have to put up with a mate's craziness?

• *"Is life really better now?"* You might question whether bailing out has made any real, fundamental changes in your life.

Michelle became overly philosophical as a consequence of bailing out, asking herself, "Has bailing out made any fundamental changes in my life? Has bailing out made my life any better? If this is all there is to life, then perhaps I should have stayed in that situation. At least I had the security of that relationship."

I offered Michelle an alternative cognition: Life is such a series of ups and downs that to demand it be much better at any particular point is unrealistic. The fact is, life is different at different points. Most likely, you will feel happier and accomplish your goals more of the time without the relationship than with the relationship. Again, there are no guarantees that you won't feel moody or that you will progress as you desire during various periods. The point is that overall the decision to bail out was a good one, although at every moment you can't expect to say, "I'm much happier now." It's just like the Dow Jones average on the stock market. Brokers advise their clients not to worry about any one particular day but to focus on the trend. Ask yourself, "What's the trend of my life like?"

Let's try to identify some other typical second thoughts.

My friends think I'm crazy, and they usually know what's good for me better than I do.
I always had money, now I'm broke. What have I done?
His lifestyle was alive and vibrant, and mine seems so boring.
Sex was so great, and now I'm not having such a good time.
Statistics say single women have a much harder time finding someone than do single men. Should I have given up a relationship that easily?

Add your own second thoughts.

Try this exercise to help you overcome your second thoughts. Identify your own particular second thoughts and write each one out on a separate index card. On the other side of each card, write down the appropriate counterthought. Possible counterthoughts for the second thoughts discussed earlier are listed on the following pages:

• *My friends think I'm crazy, and they usually know what's good for me better than I do.* Counterthought: Comfort and joy are in the eyes of the beholder. My friends are prone to the same misjudgments as I am. They are just as human and fallible as I am. They may have been raised in a way that helped them develop more patience and tolerance than me, but I am me and I can't change that.

• *I always had money, now I'm broke. What have I done?* Counterthought: How much is money really worth? I'm complaining now, but is any amount of money really worth the terrible discomfort I suffered in the relationship? Wouldn't I have paid anything to get out during the bad times? Am I really destined to be poor? Is that a realistic idea about my future? Even if I don't have the capacity or am not lucky enough to become financially secure on my own, isn't it reasonably likely that I will be able to attract another financially capable partner?

• *His lifestyle was alive and vibrant, and mine seems so boring.* Counterthought: I learned a great deal about openness and fun from him, and now I can use it to my advantage in my new life. One of the reasons he was attached to me was because he sensed I had the personality to enjoy his exciting lifestyle. Now, let me use that capacity for myself.

• *Sex was so great, and now I'm not having such a good time.* Counterthought: Where is it written that I must have the greatest orgasms any woman has ever had? It may not be wonderful with the next lover, but there's every evidence to believe that it will be pleasurable. Perhaps sex was so intensely wonderful because my partner was so unavailable and because we had nothing else going for us. Also, if I could have that kind of sexuality once, I could most likely have that level of excitement and satisfaction again.

• *Statistics say single women have a much harder time than do single men. Should I have given up a relationship that easily?* Counterthought: Statistics are easily manipulated and have little to do with how I effect my own destiny. My thoughts and behaviors have more to do with what happens in my future than do a set of percentages and figures.

Carry your cards around with you in your handbag, pocket, or briefcase, and refer to them on a regular basis, whenever you get an "uncontrollable" urge to contact your ex or whenever you feel overwhelmed by fantasies that you feel you can't control. At those moments, pull out the right card, read the counterthoughts, and try to generate additional counterthoughts.

What about the Children?

How do you use what you have learned in this book to help your children adjust to their new life? How do you employ cognitive behavior therapy to deal with your children's transition? How do you help them through their healing process? This first step is to know when your children are in trouble.

How to Spot Problems with Your Children

The following are signs that your child needs help. First and foremost, if you and your spouse are warring and using the children as pawns—that is, making conflicting decisions about the children's activities, school, friends, home life, etc., and generally not providing a solid model for problem solving—then it is very likely your children are going to have many problems.

• *Withdrawal from friends.* During his parents' bailing out period, eight-year-old Michael suddenly said he didn't like his best friend, Simon, and no longer wanted to play with him. Michael had an even more uncomfortable reaction when he was invited to his friend's house. Simon's parents were very close and spent a good deal of time with their children. At the same time he was witnessing this close-knit family, Michael was anticipating the loss of his father. The contrast was too painful and it pushed Michael into anticipatory mourning. Some children will begin to fight with their friends or burst into tears for relatively little reason.

• *Changes in personality.* Happy-go-lucky children often turn into sober, serious, sad kids. Within two months of his parents' breakup, William, age ten, changed from a happy free spirit with a reputation as the class clown, into a withdrawn, less attentive child. In class he was neglecting to do his schoolwork and was spending long hours staring out the window.

• *Regression into childlike behaviors, such as baby talk, bed-wetting, and thumb sucking.* Seven-year-old Jane had not wet her bed for three years. Soon after her parents split up, she resumed bed-wetting, a clear sign that her confusion and insecurity was causing her the kind of tension that would lead to loss of bladder control.

• *Atypical anger episodes.* Connor, twelve years old, had been reasonably happy and emotionally stable. After his mother bailed out and his father left the familial home, Connor began to blow up at his mother on a regular basis. He refused to listen to her and developed a real conduct problem in school, always getting into fights and confronting the teachers. He was angry that his parents had split and that the whole family would no longer go on summer vacation. Most of all, he was frustrated at his own sense of helplessness in the situation.

• *Compulsive behaviors.* One child spent a great deal of time zipping and unzipping his jacket and other articles of clothing in an obsessive-compulsive fashion. His odd behavior was an attempt to get attention from his mother who, because of her own fears, had been extremely distractible and neglectful of her son's needs.

• *Sleeping disorders such as nightmares, night terrors, insomnia, and interrupted sleep.* For the first week after her parents bailed out, fourteen-year-old Stephanie presented a placid, accepting attitude. She told her mother she understood her decision completely. She went to visit her father and seemed very comfortable with her new surroundings. But after that initial week, she began having trouble falling asleep. She woke up repeatedly during the night and reported a variety of nightmares that were clearly thematically related to her parents' separation.

• *Marked decrease in motivation, concentration, and achievement in school.* Ten-year-old Glen had been a straight-*A* student, the apple of every teacher's eye. Within three weeks after his parents' breakup, his school performance began to deteriorate. He wasn't paying attention in class. In fact, he frequently seemed to be in a fugue state, obsessively daydreaming.

• *Changes in eating patterns.* Sixteen-year-old Cynthia began to show clear evidence of a serious eating disorder soon after her father left home. She would eat secretly at night, covering the substantial dent she made in the family larder by taking only a certain amount of cookies from each package, or a few tablespoons of ice cream from each container, but gorging on enough food to become bloated. She would follow these bouts of stuffing herself with vomiting—a pattern of binge and purge. At other times, she would put herself on punishing starvation diets.

Whenever you spot any of these problem signs, you should immediately try to talk with the child about his behavior. First, try to get the child to acknowledge that the problem exists. Try to get the child to talk about what is on his mind. One fun way of doing this with children is the "time sampling method." Give your child a buzzer that goes off every five or ten minutes. Every time the buzzer goes off, have your child write down what he is thinking, or, if the child is very young, have him talk about his feelings. That is one way to get a sample of the kinds of things that are worrying your child.

Frequently, your child won't tell you what is bothering him, so, in effect, you have to tell him. You can say, "Look, Mommy is really concerned about the fact that Daddy isn't living here anymore." Or "I'm really concerned that Mommy and Daddy have split up. It's been keeping me up nights. Has it been keeping you up nights too?" Sharing your own vulnerability often reassures your child that his own feelings are not odd and he doesn't have to be ashamed of them. Hearing that you share the same feelings validates your child's feelings. You can also say to your child, "You know, if I were you, I would be really angry." That allows your child to feel that anger is okay. You can even say, "If I were you, there would be times I would want to beat my daddy up or even beat me up! And I can really understand that." Do whatever you can to get your child to acknowledge what is going on inside. You can also use any of the techniques for helping children described in chapter 6.

You also must be sensitive to any cognitive distortions your child has, such as overmagnifying, perfectionism in his demands about his environment and himself, and catastrophizing the situation. Arm yourself with replacement cognitions that you can help him begin to integrate.

If all fails and you can't get your child to acknowledge and work on his feelings and to reach some sort of cognitive resolutions, then visit a therapist.

Dating Again

How do you begin to go out again? How do you make that initial connection?

The following techniques will make dating again less like the *Perils of Pauline* and more of a *Great Adventure*.

Positive Time Projection

At this stage in the bailing-out process, the use of the "positive time projection" technique is valuable. It is extremely important to generate positive visualizations.

Enter a state of relaxation, using the techniques you learned in chapter 5. One at a time, imagine yourself at different time periods starting from the present: three months from now, six months from now, one year from now, etc. Imagine different scenes involving different aspects of dating at each time period—some good, some shaky, but during each time projection always seeing yourself coping with confidence.

One scene might be three months from now. You are receiving a telephone call from a man. You are upbeat and confident. Another scene might involve a blind date who presents himself at your door. Your fantasies that "this will be the one" are shattered when you first see him because he isn't "your type." See yourself getting past that initial negative reaction, getting to know this man as a person, enjoying his acquaintance, really listening to him and not imposing on him your expectations that he be Prince Charming. The two of you share a pleasant evening.

Another possibility might be to imagine yourself having a date with a man on whom you've had a crush for two months. You are finally having dinner with him. You are not intimidated or overwhelmed because you like him so much. You are simply enjoying this opportunity to get to know him better.

If you discover that while doing these positive visualizations, you begin to resist feeling confident and have difficulty seeing yourself coping well, try to identify exactly what self-defeating or distorted thoughts are gumming up the works. Then, take time out to challenge these thoughts with alternative, healthy thoughts and get on with your confidence building.

Finding Creative Ways to Meet People

One woman asked an older grandmotherly type who seemed
eager to dispense good advice to everyone, "Where are all the
good men?" "In the cemetery!" the old woman responded.

Despite this sage's opinion, there are still quite a few good
men lurking about. It is important at this stage in the bailing-
out process that you find creative ways of meeting new people. They are out there. Seize every opportunity available.
Most people want to meet other people, but they are often as
shy and reluctant as you are. The following are just a few
suggestions of what you might do. Go into these situations
with the idea that you are going to meet new people.

• *You can write personal ads for yourself even if you do
not actually place them.* What kinds of ads would you write
to promote yourself? What do you want to say about the kind
of person you have become as a consequence of the separation
or divorce? Write an ad presenting yourself as you were when
you first entered your old relationship. Then write another ad
presenting yourself as you are now. There's often a time lag in
our images of ourselves. We tend to see ourselves today not as
we really are but as we were several years ago. Compare the
two ads. What do they say about the changes that have taken
place in you and about how you view yourself? Comparing the
two ads can help you see the growth you have made.

If you do decide to actually place the ad, do not burden
yourself with expectations that your ad be the cleverest, most
enticing notice in the paper. This does not have to be the Great
American Singles Ad. Just be straightforward, positive, and
accurate about who you are and who you are looking for. The
personal page editors are usually very happy to help you write
the appropriate copy. Be sure, however, to meet your dates in
public places to avoid any possible danger.

• *You can go to various lectures, presentations, or seminars in your town.* Give yourself the assignment of talking for
at least a few seconds to the people to the left and right of

you. Chances are that because you all attended the same function, you have that and other interests in common. After these kinds of programs, people frequently get together to discuss the presentation. See if you can join or even start such a group. People are usually eager to discuss their experience; they just need a catalyst to do so.

• *Sign up at a health club.* Not only will you get in better shape, but there are sure to be many men ready to appreciate it. Conversation is easily struck up in such a setting. You can always ask for help with equipment or query someone on how a particular exercise is done.

• *Parents Without Partners is a well-established organization through which you can meet people who share your responsiblity of children.* If you have problems with finding or affording baby-sitting services, you can plan activities with your new friends that involve both your children.

• *Go to museums and art galleries.* Join one of the floating tours so that you can talk easily with the other people on the tour. People are eager to share their knowledge and insights about what they are viewing; be an active, appreciative listener.

• *Volunteer for a political campaign.* A number of my patients have dated people in this way because they have met someone with a common interest. During the final phases of political campaigns the spirit of camaraderie intensifies, a perfect setting for romance.

• *In urban areas, co-op committees in apartment buildings are wonderful ways to meet people, particularly in cities where you often do not know your neighbors.*

• *Take a class in a subject that interests you.* If it interests you, then anyone you meet in class obviously shares your interest. You might check ahead with the teacher to see if there are small-group activities. The best way to get to know someone in class is by working with him.

• *The specialized singles dating services are a good idea.* These include services for classical music lovers, pet lovers, and chess lovers. Once again, you are put in contact with people who share your interests.

• *Work can always be an opportunity for meeting new people.* Although office romances can be tricky to negotiate, working together can help the two of you to understand each other. Any relationship that begins on that basis has a good chance of succeeding.

• *Personal telephone dialogues are sweeping the country.* These differ from party lines. In personal telephone dialogues, you place an ad and are given an extension number. If you find an ad that interests you, you can call the telephone and extension numbers given to hear a message from the man describing himself. Then, if you wish, you can leave a personal message for that person. Many of my patients have met and dated through these services. Once again, exercise caution in meeting these dates.

• *I've had patients who met people while looking for an apartment.* In fact, I have assigned some people to go out on the weekend and look for an apartment. I tell them, "While you are looking for an apartment, you will be with other single people looking for an apartment. Your assignment is to start up a conversation."

Now list your own ideas. There are many places where you can easily connect with someone. Give yourself the assignment of trying at least one new method of meeting people per week. Stipulate that you do not leave the situation until you talk to at least one person.

If you are shy, the following techniques have proven helpful in overcoming the problem of approaching new people. Go to a supermarket and strike up a conversation with someone. You can ask where the fruit section is, and when the person answers, you can respond with a comment about the supermarket or the fruit. The idea here is to gradually extend each conversation. First, talk for ten seconds, then for twenty seconds, and then build up to a minute.

You can start a conversation in an elevator with the person standing next to you. "Boy, is this slow" or "It's warm in here," are obvious possibilities. Try to smile at people on the street.

Offer spontaneous compliments to people you meet during the day. Another good idea is to have a stockpile of entertaining or interesting anecdotes you can call on at a social event whenver you feel at a loss for words. *How to Start a Conversation and make Friends,* by Don Gabor, is a valuable source for chronically shy people.

All of the above strategies are designed to reduce your shyness. Most shy people experience what we call "fear of negative evaluation." They fear that if they put themselves forward they will be judged harshly as foolish, dull, ignorant, and generally socially unacceptable. But by repeatedly challenging that fear through engaging in social interaction, the evidence becomes overwhelming that people are not really sitting in such negative judgment of you.

What Do You Tell a New Date?

How do you achieve the fine balance between being too open and being withholding? If you pour forth your feelings about your former relationship and the breakup too soon, you will turn the person off because he will feel you are too caught up in your past relationship and you're never going to work it through. If you withhold information, it will seem to him that you are in anguish and don't really want to be with him. You have to find a good balance between the two extremes. Timing is everything in terms of how much you reveal to a new date. Getting to know someone is like peeling the skin of an onion away. You peel the outer layer off first by talking about the weather. On the next level, you discuss your opinions on more personal subjects. Finally, when you get to the core, you talk about your intimate feelings, your dreams, your fears, and your past. With some people the process moves quickly and it is reciprocal. Other people may not want to share themselves or hear about you on such a personal level. You must learn to be sensitive to what the other person is about.

Here are some sample statements you might make and questions you might ask your dates in your attempt to determine how much you want to share.

"Listen, how much do you really want to hear about my previous relationship?" With this question, you are giving the other person the responsibility for determining how much he wants to hear.

"Will knowing more about me make you more comfortable?" This also opens the door for the person to signal whether or not he wants to hear about your past relationship.

"This is very uncomfortable for me, but I think it's useful to get my feelings off my chest."

"I think it's too early in our relationship to bring up past relationships. Don't you agree?"

"I know I've talked a lot about my past relationship, but you seemed to be genuinely interested."

In general, be straightforward and honest and be alert to the signals you are getting from the other person as to how much they need and want to hear about your past.

What About Sex?

What do you do the first time a new person touches you? First of all, you have to accept the feelings of confusion and sadness you're likely to have when you begin to make love with somebody new or when he begins to reach out to you. For example, if you're a woman, your first thought might be, "My God, that's not the way Bill used to touch me!" Or "How am I ever going to teach men to touch me the way Bill used to touch me?" Or "This is no better than sex with Bill. I might as well be with him." Then the old fears flood back, exaggerated and overwhelming: "*Nobody* is *ever* going to touch me that way." "I'm going to have to train somebody new. It's going to take a whole lifetime." "I'm going to be without love, without sex." "My indifferent sex life is my fault. I will never be satisfied with anyone."

The first experiences are going to push all those buttons. The key here is honesty. You've got to be able to talk about it. Some of my patients have reported feeling awkward but they have learned to express their feelings to new people using the following statements:

"Please understand I'm very sensitive about sex. It's going to take time and tenderness before I'm ready."
"I'm just not able to be responsive right now. Please bear with me. What I need is tenderness and understanding."
"I feel sad because when I feel sexual toward you, it reminds me of how I turned off in my other relationship. But I'm sure it will pass."

Research reported in a recent issue of *The Journal of Personality and Social Psychology* found that what men most resent about women is their lack of response to sexual advances, whereas women resent men's tendency to be overly sexual and to play down expressions of tenderness and understanding. Communication about each other's needs helps to bridge this gender gap.

Coping with Tender Feelings about the Past Relationship

Tender feelings are normal. You must not feel guilty or put yourself down for having these tender feelings.

Miserable Memory List

All throughout the period of initial separation, you should be creating a "miserable memory list," a catalog of reminders of all the negative things that happened in the relationship. Again, human nature resists doing that. Human nature forgets all the bad parts, particularly if you are feeling lonely, detached, and disconnected. Keep referring to the list when the going gets really bad. It is equally important to compile a positive memory list to remind yourself that the relationship was not a total loss. But save that list for later, after you have passed through that initial phase of separation when you might be overwhelmed by regrets and shortcircuit the bailing-out process.

One patient referred to the list of miserable memories as her "package." Every time she began to experience those tender feelings, she would pull out her list and ask herself, "Do I really want this entire package?" She reminded herself that it was not only the tender memories she would buy into but the entire package.

Tell Your Diary Instead

You can cope with tender feelings about the past relationship by talking about these feelings as much as possible to a neutral party. Even better, write about these feelings when you are home. Write about what you felt. It is very important to externalize these feelings, to get them outside of yourself and to demystify them.

Every time Stephanie went out with a new man, she would remember how Bill used to treat her. She'd remember the poems he would write her, and so on. A new date obviously could not compare, in terms of level of intimacy and comfort, with her ex-partner. By using the diary, she was able to control the tendency to forget the bad and be overwhelmed by nostalgic feelings.

Comparisons

Resist as much as possible the temptation to compare these new people with your former partner. Whenever you find yourself comparing, you can use a simple technique such as "thought stopping." In thought stopping, you simply say stop to yourself. Put a little rubber band around your wrist and as soon as you find yourself comparing the new people to your former partner, snap the rubber band and say to yourself, "No, I'll wait until my comparing hour."

Make a kind of appointment with yourself to do all your comparing at a certain time, such as five o'clock in the afternoon. You cannot stop the human mind from having a thought. You are not going to stop comparing, but you can delay these thoughts and not get bogged down in these comparisons while you are out on a date and certain to ruin the experience.

The following steps represent the suggested procedure for thought stopping. Before you begin, slip a rubber band around your wrist.

First, imagine your ex-lover compared to the new person. The past partner compares much more favorably than the new partner.

Second, say stop out loud and snap the rubber band that's around your wrist.

Third, drop the scene from your mind.

Fourth, switch to a "relief thought," an alternative thought that is not associated with the ex-lover. It could be a pleasant scene involving the new person or an image of relaxing with your friends.

Essentially, you are punishing nostalgic thoughts about your ex with the rubber band and rewarding stopping the thought with the new image.

The key here is to rehearse thought stopping. Do not wait for comparison thoughts to come into your mind. Sit down and create comparison thoughts. Have a stockpile of alternative thoughts ready for the reward phase.

Remember: Nostalgic thoughts are not always bad. They can be useful when you have the need to soothe yourself with memories of good times. But they don't have a place of honor when you are developing new relationships.

Role-Playing

Another strategy to cope with the discomfort of being with new people is to role-play with friends. Have your friend play you. In this role reversal, your friend voices your feelings about your ex. You play your friend or your more conscious self and counter with all the reasons why you are no longer with this person and why the breakup does not have to be ugly and bitter. If you are stuck for reasons, refer to your miserable memory list.

Another variation is the Gestalt "empty chair" technique. Sit in a chair opposite an empty chair. Imagine the empty chair contains your old feelings. Talk to those feelings from your realistic, practical point of view. Get up and move to the other chair and let those feelings respond. Continue the dialogue until the tender feelings have been given outlet and have been fully countered by your practical, realistic self. This exercise puts people in touch with what they are really feeling and allows them to gain some control of their less aware points of view.

Should You Date Your Ex?

The answer is no, unless that's part of a therapeutic arrangement designed with the goal of reconciliation. It's generally bad business to start dating again. The old adage that you can't go home again should stick here. Dating your ex merely pushes old buttons. In addition, you're seeing the old person in a new and relaxed context. That's very dangerous because there are none of the old stresses. You are on your best behavior, he is on his best behavior. You're living apart, you've both forgotten each other's annoying little traits, and you're both trying to get things back together. If you're certain you bailed out forever, it does very little good to maintain the relationship.

Jill tried to convince me soon after she had bailed out that her ex was still her very best friend. This is a fairly pervasive problem. "Even though he can't be my lover," people ask, "Why do I have to drop him from my life completely?" In fact, you don't always have to. Many people do continue with a friendship, but some can handle it and others cannot. You have to ask yourself if both of you can cope with that kind of relationship. Can you keep your hands off each other? Do you have enough common interests? Are both your egos strong enough to bear seeing the other person date others? You have to do a lot of soul-searching before you conclude that he can be your best friend.

Jill did go out with her ex, convinced that they wouldn't sleep together, that they would just be friends. Within a month, they started sleeping together, and it was disastrous. Jill fell right back into the relationship and her ex continued to be the same unambitious, emotionally unavailable toadstool he had been before. Jill was forced to undergo the entire bailing-out process all over again. In retrospect, she realized that, yes, perhaps she had more in common with this man than with anyone else, but that didn't mean she should have a relationship with him. I pointed out to her that there were thousands of people in America with whom she could have wonderful relationships, but she didn't know any of them yet. This man did not have to be designated as the "only one."

CONCLUSION

Since we began this book, more and more men and women have entered therapy reporting a variety of symptoms, including anxiety, depression, obsessive worrying, and phobias as well as obvious relationship problems. After exploring these symptoms, many of these complaints seem related to feelings of being trapped in unsatisfying relationships.

The courageous people are those who have been willing to follow the strategies outlined for them—strategies that are included in this book. They are often rewarded with a genuine cessation in symptoms.

We are not certain why more and more people feel trapped in unrewarding relationships. Perhaps a variety of social forces are exerting more pressure to remain in a couple situation. Numerous articles have recently been published on the high cost of divorce. The tremendous increase in palimony suits may also keep people stuck, even when they know they should move on. The AIDS epidemic is more of a threat than ever, with potentially fruitful research seemingly reaching dead ends. The media extolls us to be assertive with new partners—something many of us do not have the capacity to do—and, at the same time, we are told to remain monogamous and not to be experimental. Fear continues to grip us and keep us stuck in unfulfilling relationships. New books and research scare us as we become more aware of the deleterious effect on the children of divorce, especially when the partners continue to war with each other and do not set good problem-solving examples. So we remain stuck out of guilt, shame, and social pressure.

Social pressure also occurs when we read statistics on the dismal chances of remarriage or even of finding a good relationship as we get older, and so we conclude it's better to hold on to what we have, no matter how miserable we are. The conservative atmosphere of the current administration with its emphasis on traditional family values is another pressure that keeps many of us stuck in unhappy relationships. Perhaps the biggest problem, however, is what we have called the Sand Castle Syndrome. A couple may have built an entire lifetime together—raising children, buying a home, developing friendships—and they just can't see tearing it down. As the world becomes a more technical and inhumane place, we tend all the more to draw together for security and comfort, even if these bonds are based on a weak foundation.

As all these pressures encouraging couples to stay together increase, so do the shame and guilt about wanting to bail out. There is an obvious need for a corrective measure to all these pressures, and this book aims to fill that need. We want to assure you that, in many cases, bailing out is not only okay, but the best possible alternative.

As we were writing the closing sentences of this book, Dr. Lubetkin received a telephone call from a patient he had last seen five years ago. Much of what is in this book was inspired by courageous patients like Janis who overcame fears and insecurities about leaving their partners. Janis still recalls her disbelief and lack of confidence when she began therapy. She simply couldn't believe that she would ever be able to bail out. Through consistent effort, Janis was able to completely change her thinking. She was able to make a clear, rational decision to bail out, and she accomplished this with a minimum of discomfort to herself and her partner. Through hard work it is my hope that you too will benefit from the action plan that is the heart of this book. I cannot guarantee a perfect landing, but bailing out may save your life.

INDEX

Rules and guidelines (*cont.*)
  on task rules, 164–65
  for trial separation, 163–65
  see also Exercises

S

Sadness after bailing out, 190
Safety net, 60–61, 62–63, 159–62
Sand castle syndrome, 127, 216
Sarcasm, screening regarding, 93
Scapegoat, relationship as, 124–25
School problems with children, 201
Screening, 73–99
  about children, 91
  about early parenting, 80–84
  about family problems, 85–86
  about gifts, 86–88
  about humor, 92–93
  about partner's friends, 88–89
  about past breakups, 78–80
  about past relationships, 76–80
  about pets, 91
  about quality time, 89–90
  about responsibility, 90–91
  about sharing feelings, 93–94
  necessity of, 73–74
  rationalizations about, 74–76, 95
  screening weekend, 95–99
  therapy as, 98–99
  when to screen, 76
Second thoughts, 194–99
Secretiveness, 45
Security, 70, 122, 183, 198
Seductiveness, as cry for help, 61–62
Self-denigration, 196
Self-help books, exercises in, 15–17
Self-identity
  contingent self-acceptance, 106–7
  love slobs and, 102–5
  marraige and, 32
  vicarious modeling and, 107–8
  "who I am" vs. "what I do", 105–6
Separation, trial, 163–66
Serial relationships, 13–14

Sex
  dating again and, 208–9
  as reason for relationships, 68–69
  second thoughts concerning, 198
  trial separations and, 165
  as warning sign, 48–49
Shame attack exercises, 147
Shyness, overcoming, 206–7
Single life, preparing for, 182–85
Single-parent family, 83–84
Single relationships, 29–31
Single women, 198–99
Sleeping disorders, 200–201
Social learning theory, 9–11
Spouse. *See* Partner
Stability, emotional, 71–72
Standard of living, 122, 183, 198
Static. *See* Mental static
Subjective units of disturbance scale
    (SUDS), 143–45
Suicidal partner, leaving, 168–70
Suicide gestures, 61
Systematic desensitization, 134–35,
    142–46

T

Tachycardia. *See* Anxiety
Techniques. *See* Exercises; Rules and
    guidelines
Telephone dialogues, personal, 206
Tension-release relaxation technique,
    137–39, 141–42
Therapists
  aversion to separation among, 7
  credentials for, 59
  evaluating, 57–60
  help with bailing out from, 162–63
  suicidal partner and, 169–70
  see also Martial counseling
Thought stopping, 211–12
Thumb sucking, 200
Timing
  for bail out, 6–7, 33, 41–65, 157–58
  positive time projection, 203

ABOUT THE AUTHORS

Dr. Barry Lubetkin is the cofounder and clinical director of the Institute for Behavior Therapy in New York City, one of the largest and most-comprehensive treatment centers of its kind in the country. He is currently the president of the American Board of Behavioral Psychology and a diplomate in Clinical Psychology from the American Board of Professional Psychology.

Dr. Lubetkin is considered a leading spokesman in the emerging field of cognitive behavior therapy. His scientific insights and therapeutic wisdom have been communicated widely to both professional and lay audiences. In addition to numerous scientific articles and chapters, his work has been featured in such publications as *Cosmopolitan*, *Glamour*, *Vogue*, *New York Magazine*, *Playgirl*, *Redbook*, the New York *Daily News*, the New York *Post*, *Prevention*, *Boardroom Reports*, and many others. He has spoken on radio talk shows numerous times and was a featured psychologist for several years on "The Leon Lewis Show" on WMCA talk radio. He has been interviewed on a variety of television shows in the New York area including the nationally syndicated "Joan Lunden Show."

Dr. Lubetkin received his Ph.D. from Kent State University in 1969. He spent the next year at Massachusetts General Hospital and Harvard Medical School as a National Institute of Mental Health postdoctoral fellow. The following year he was a postdoctoral fellow in behavior modification at the State University of New York at Stony Brook. Over the last two decades he has held senior clinical supervisory positions and teaching positions at a number of prestigious institutions, including New York University Medical Center, Bellevue Psychiatric Hospital, Rutgers University Graduate School, Institute for Rational Emotive Therapy, and Hofstra University.

Dr. Lubetkin lives in New York City with his wife, Ginny, and their two children.

Dr. Elena Oumano is a university professor of communications theory and practice, the author of four books, and a freelance journalist.

For the last eighteen years, Dr. Oumano has taught interpersonal communications, communications media, public speaking, and communications theory at various colleges within the City University of New York system.

Dr. Oumano is the author of the following books: *Film Forum* (St. Martin's Press, 1985), *Sam Shepard* (St. Martin's Press, 1986), *Movies for a Desert Isle* (St. Martin's Press, 1987), and *Paul Newman* (St. Martin's Press, 1989). She was a regular music journalist for *TAXI*; writes a weekly article on African and Caribbean music for *The City Sun;* and has written other articles on health, relationships, music, and film for numerous other magazines.

Dr. Oumano has worked as an actress, writer, and technician on independent theater and film projects and has appeared as a regular guest interviewer on the "John and Johanna Show" on cable television.

Dr. Oumano received her Ph.D. in language and communications in 1979 from New York University. She has studied psychoanalysis at the Institute for Modern Analysis in New

York City and has received certifications in counseling, yoga teaching, and body work from the Kripalu Health Center in Lenox, Massachusetts.

Dr. Oumano lives in New York City.